S0-AFN-245

Experiences
From
the Light

Ordinary People's Extraordinary Experiences of
Transformation, Miracles, and Spiritual Awakening

Experiences From the Light

KEIDI KEATING

New Page Books
A division of the Career Press, Inc.
Pompton Plains, N.J.

Copyright © 2015 by Keidi Keating

All rights reserved under the Pan-American and International Copyright Conventions. This book may not be reproduced, in whole or in part, in any form or by any means electronic or mechanical, including photocopying, recording, or by any information storage and retrieval system now known or hereafter invented, without written permis-sion from the publisher, The Career Press.

Experiences From the Light
Edited and Typeset by Kara Kumpel
Cover design by Howard Grossman/12E Design
Printed in the U.S.A.

Contribution by Brian Longhurst originally published by Six Degrees Publishing Group, used by permission.

To order this title, please call toll-free 1-800-CAREER-1 (NJ and Canada: 201-848-0310) to order using VISA or MasterCard, or for further information on books from Career Press.

The Career Press, Inc.
220 West Parkway, Unit 12
Pompton Plains, NJ 07444
www.careerpress.com
www.newpagebooks.com

Library of Congress Cataloging-in-Publication Data
CIP Data Available Upon Request.

This book is dedicated to Infinite Love, a nonprofit organization founded by Pooja Chugani, Alka Vaswani, Malka Shivdasani, and Geeta Thadani. The book has been compiled and published in loving memory of the cousin of these four women, Vishal Buxani, who passed away from cancer on February 14, 2011 (Valentine's Day), at the age of 30.

Vishal, you're a shining Light for us all!

At least 10 percent of the net profit from royalties of this book will be donated to Infinite Love for the wonderful work they do for homeless people and cancer patients in their community.

Acknowledgments

I'd like to say thank you to many people for assisting with the compilation of this book, including all of the contributors who made *Experiences from the Light* possible.

But I'm going to say an extra-special thank-you to John-Roger, my spiritual teacher who passed away on October 20, 2014, at the age of 80. J-R, thank you for your Light-filled blessings and for appearing in my dreams with profound messages. You are in all of our hearts.

Contents

Preface   11

Chapter 1: Seeing the Light   13

Chapter 2: Spiritual Awakenings   37

Chapter 3: Messages from Spirit/Synchronicity   87

Chapter 4: Birds, Animals, and Other Creatures,
             Great and Small   101

Chapter 5: Seeing Spirit   113

Chapter 6: Jesus and the Masters   127

Chapter 7: Protected by Spirit and Angels   151

Chapter 8: Premonitions   163

Chapter 9: Healing   169

Chapter 10: Past Lives   181

Chapter 11: Subtle Experiences   203

Chapter 12: Out-of-Body Experiences   225

Index   243

About the Author   247

Preface

Not long after the launch of *The Light: A Book of Wisdom*, something peculiar started to happen. Everywhere I went, from airports to supermarkets, restaurants to elevators, random strangers would open their hearts and tell me their mystical experiences and transformational stories of Spirit and the other side. At times, these stories were instigated by my own true life tales, told with heartfelt passion and enthusiasm, but on other occasions, people would regale me with their stories on a whim, with no prompting on my part. Generally, no one had any idea who I was. They didn't know that I was a spiritual author, who had put together a book called *The Light* with contributions by 22 luminaries to help people reawaken their own Divine inner spark.

And so I felt rather like a giant human magnet to which people were attracted in order to finally tell these suppressed stories.

In the past, many of us feared being ridiculed if we let these stories escape into the judgmental eyes and ears of the public domain. Thankfully that is no longer the case, as a greater number of us are awakening to the fact that there is most definitely something more than this dense, materialistic planet called Earth. My purpose, as a bridge between worlds, is to bring these inspiring stories to Light and shine unto everyone the message that we are not our bodies, that we live beyond our life here on Earth, that we have reincarnated hundreds, if not thousands of times, and that loving is the most important lesson we are here to learn. Thanks to all those random strangers who told me their stories, I quickly realized that Spirit wanted me to bring out another Light book: *Experiences from the Light*. And so I began gathering these stories, taking down the name and contact details of those who courageously told their true life experiences. My true wish is that, by reading the many stories inside this book, you shine even brighter, remember your own spiritual experiences with an open heart, and shed the fear of sharing them with others.

And if you have not yet experienced such magical happenings for yourself, then my desire is that this book will open a door for you, so you can discover your own faith and belief in these miraculous occurrences.

Continue spreading the word at the same time as sowing your love so that we may unite and bathe in the glory and grace of the Light's everlasting presence.

Loving you dearly and sending Light-filled blessings your way...

Keidi Keating
xxx

Chapter 1:
Seeing the Light

People often comment that they have "finally seen the Light" after enduring a prolonged spell of depression or heartache, commonly known as "the dark night of the soul." In such cases, this means that something happened in their life which led them to reveal their true selves again, and live from that special space of Truth and beauty. However, there are also people who have quite literally *seen* the Light in all of its innate glory!

In the aftermath of my 12 months of depression, I saw a huge ball of Light in my bedroom as I awoke in the early hours of the morning. I can still see the scene clearly now. The ball of Light was large and oval-shaped, and as it hovered between the ceiling and the floor, a strange, muffled sound emanated from it. I knew it was trying to tell me some important information. The next day a message landed in my head telling me to bring out a book containing chapters by all of the people who had helped me to find my own Light. I'm convinced that is exactly what the orb of Light had been trying to tell me.

Another night, soon after I began cellular healing sessions, I awoke to a very surreal and peculiar sight. A translucent green-colored code of Light, consisting of numbers, letters, and obscure symbols drifted towards me and then passed directly into my being. It felt as if something unearthly was being downloaded into me. In fact, it had an alien quality about it. The next morning, as I awoke, I had an ocean in my awareness, and I found myself sending out this vast body of water Love and Light. I wondered whether I'd received a new DNA code during the night. After I told a few people about this experience, others divulged that a similar code had been downloaded into them too.

The more I spoke to people about their experiences, the more surprised (and amazed) I became. All of the stories about **Seeing the Light** in this section are absolutely beautiful. It amazes me what is possible for us humans when we truly and wholeheartedly believe; after all, it's not "seeing is believing" but "believing is seeing," and if you would like to see the Light too, then read that last sentence again!

HEATHER WADE GREEN

Teacher and Coach for Women,
Mill Valley, California, United States

Move Towards the Light

I would like to share the life and death of my beloved grand-mother, Nanny. To try and tell you how it feels to stand in the sunshine of her love is like trying to describe the ceiling of the Sistine Chapel, or the feeling of holding your new baby for the first time. But I will do my best. And hopefully, by the end of this story you too will feel the sunshine of her love warm your soul.

Because my dad was rarely in my life and my mother suffered from severe health issues, my mother and I lived with my grand-parents until I went to college. Nanny was like a second mother to me and considered me her daughter.

I was born with lung disease and spent much of the first two years of my life in hospital. Chronic illness plagued me from child-hood to young adulthood. I was on antibiotics from the age of 15 and suffered from daily seizures. But in a miraculous twist of fate, I eventually overcame the illness and went on to finish 7th in my age group in an Iron Man triathlon. I am confident that this happened for three reasons: 1) my grandmother taught me that miracles happen every day; 2) she prayed to the Virgin Mary regularly; 3) she reinforced the fact that I was safe, loved, and protected.

I believe Nanny literally saved my life. Besides having a hand in my physical healing, she kept me "good" when I almost went down the wrong path. Having a sick mother and being abandoned by my father sometimes left me unsupervised, depressed, and wild, but Nanny's special love kept me from crossing over to the dark side.

Growing up, I often thought about the day she would die and how I would ever make it through that. I couldn't think of anything worse than living in this world without her.

For years, Nanny would make silly mistakes and her forgetfulness would make my high school friends and me laugh. Her Alzheimer's had been with us for years before we gave it a name. In 2003, a few years after I finished college, I moved to Spain. During that year Nanny took a turn for the worse. When I came home to visit a year later, I noticed that her Alzheimer's had become a problem. She was constantly confused and didn't remember people. It was no longer laughable; it was a little scary. But she was still full of love. Even when she was super confused and didn't recognize other people, she always knew me. Her eyes would light up and she would hold my hand. In 2004, I decided to move back to the States to be closer to my family during this difficult time.

The following years were long and cruel. Life was not as kind to my grandmother as it should have been. She was known in the community for bringing healing and miracles to those she prayed over and now she was not really living, but simply existing, and there was no one there to heal her. Nanny was slipping away from us. Eventually she lost her ability to communicate at all and spent most of the time slumped over in her nursing home wheelchair drooling on herself. She wore diapers and her teeth were rotting; an undignified way for my beautiful grandmother to die.

Whenever I visited her, I hoped that her hazel eyes would shimmer at me. I would pray for a moment of recognition; sometimes I got it, sometimes not. When I didn't, it felt so painful. For many years she had recognized only me and when that shimmer faded it seemed there was nothing but light left in her soul.

Every time I traveled from California to the nursing home in Connecticut, my mother and other family members would tell me to say a real goodbye to Nanny, "just in case." This made sense, and for years I did that. Well, I went through the motion, but deep in my soul, every time I said goodbye, I knew her life was not over. I knew her soul would communicate with my soul from all the way across the country and let me know when to come home.

One day I received a text message from my cousin, Brett. I was sitting in class and it simply said, "Nan is not doing well." I hurried out of class and into the English office where I called my mom and then my husband. I was confused about what to do as I left school and picked up my toddler from daycare. My husband was away, but I knew I needed to go. He flew home late that Friday night so I could take the first flight out of town the next day. I took a taxi from San Francisco to Oakland at about 4 o'clock in the morning so I could fly across the country and make it to Connecticut by dinnertime. I had a layover in Middle America, so I called home and spoke to my aunt. She was crying when she answered the phone and it took a minute to compose herself. She explained that the priest had given my grandmother her last rights and that she did not have a lot of time left.

"What, you mean I am not going to make it?" I asked. She replied, "She is ready to go, but she will wait for you." In my heart, I felt exactly the same way. I boarded my second flight and it arrived more than an hour early. As the plane touched down the pilot informed us of an insane tailwind that had caused the extra speed. I remembered the words of one of my former students as I was running out of class the day before. He simply said, "Godspeed."

A family member picked me up from the airport and brought me to my mother's house. I threw my suitcase in the back of her car, and drove us both to Nanny's nursing home. When we got there my grandmother was sound asleep. She hadn't been awake in days, but the second I walked in, dragging my suitcase, I saw her head and eyes follow me from one side of the room to the next; instinctively, she knew I was there. The magnetic connection between her heart and mine awoke her.

When I reached the bed I took her hand in mine and our eyes fixed on one another. A current of intense love energy flowed between us. It was a magical feeling that I will never forget. From the minute we touched, one thing came to mind to say to her: "Move towards the light. When you see the light, move towards the light."

I am not sure where these words had come from. I said the sentence over and over in my mind and I know her soul could hear.

I never said the words out loud. There was no need for words in this state of grace. We were communicating without words and she told me everything I needed to hear. Her message was love. My two hands held one of her hands, and her other hand slowly made its way over. I couldn't let go of her hands, or tear my eyes away from her gaze. We were locked like that for hours. Finally, I asked my mother to sit in my place and to hold her hands as I pulled mine away. My phone had been ringing endlessly with family members calling and I needed to answer.

I stepped out to make a quick call, and when I returned my grandmother's eyes were closed. She lived for another few days, but that was the last time her eyes were ever really open. What I experienced that night was a gift from God and something I will never forget. I am not sure if that was the best moment of my life, or if what happened a few days later was the ultimate gift. They both offered me the opportunity to step out of this world and into heaven. Twice in one week, I stepped into the light.

I left the nursing home that night high on the experience, feeling the deepest connection I have ever felt. In the morning I returned to the nursing home with my mother. My aunt was there too. Nanny was predeceased by her son, my uncle Bobby, and my grandfather Pop, but she had her three girls with her: me, my mom, and my aunt.

Nurses came in and out of her room throughout the morning. I continued holding her hand, silently willing her to "move towards the light." Even though she never opened her eyes again, during the course of the day she repeatedly reached her hand up toward the sky, as if she saw something, or was asking someone to pull her over. A silent prayer arose in my heart and I asked my deceased grandfather and uncle to pull her over.

Around midmorning, a new nurse walked into the room. Without acknowledging us she ran right over to my grandmother, affectionately took her hands, and in a commanding voice told her, "Renee, when you see the light, move towards the light." My jaw almost dropped onto the floor. They were the exact words that I had been silently chanting to Nanny for the last 24 hours. How did she know to deliver that message too? She turned and asked us to leave the room so she could check my grandmother's vital signs. I found this strange, because all the other nurses had done this in front of us, but I trusted her so we left the room. When she came back, she said to my mother and me, "You can go back in, but before you do I need to tell you something. She accidentally knocked her IV out; her only source of food, fluids, and nutrients." I didn't believe her for a minute. My grandmother didn't have enough strength for that, but I didn't say a word because I knew it was the right thing. She said, "I think we should leave it out. If you agree, I will call the hospice and her doctor." I looked at my mom and told her it was the right thing to do. I felt that I was there for two reasons: to help my grandmother with her transition and to support my mother through this difficult life event. It took all of my mother's strength, but she agreed and we gave the nurse our blessing.

A couple of hours later, hospice nurses came to meet my mother, my aunt, and me. They told us that my grandmother would start to decline immediately, but it may take a few days for her to pass. I told them that Nanny kept reaching her hand up towards the heavens and I asked the hospice workers why. They told me that was very common. Old people do that when they see someone they love on the other side, or when they see the light. I was certain that both things were true for my Nanny; that Uncle Bobby and Poppy were waiting for her and that this holy woman did indeed see the Light of God.

I decided to spend the night with Nanny after everyone else went home. I didn't want her to be alone. The day shift had been easy because she was peaceful and I could see that she was ready, asking to cross the threshold. But by the evening she had changed. She was no longer reaching up to heaven. Her body was jolting forward as she gasped for air and the death rattle began. In the middle of the night, the nurses came in and told me Nanny's body was still very strong and it would probably be a few days before she passed, so I should go home, get a decent night's sleep, and return in the morning. I knew I needed to preserve my energy for the days ahead, so I took their advice and went to my aunt's house to rest for a few hours before returning a little later.

Thankfully, by morning the horrible death-rattle sound had subsided. Nanny seemed peaceful again, but she no longer reached up to the light.

My mother and aunt joined me at the nursing home that morning, along with my grandmother's best friend, Sheila, who was in Nanny's prayer group and had been on many religious pilgrimages with her. Sheila's stay was brief and involved lots of prayer. My mother couldn't stay in the room for long because it was too emotional for her. She kept heading out to make phone calls, or sit outside and smoke a cigarette. My aunt left in the afternoon as well. So it was just Nanny and me again. I continued to say a silent prayer to my Uncle Bobby and Poppy, asking them to take her hand and help pull her over. I continued to say, "Move towards the light. When you see the light, move towards the light."

It was just me, Nanny, and those words for the next few hours. I kept looking outside her window at the barren earth. It was November in Connecticut and I was filled with a general feeling of emptiness; my soul was chilled as I watched the last day I had with her fade away. It felt like time was moving so slowly and I wanted to savor every moment, but I also wanted it to be over, for her to hurry up and reach the finish line. I paid attention to the light fading from the sky as dusk set in, and somehow I was in perfect communication with God. I knew Nanny's life was slipping away with the daylight and that they were in perfect synchronicity.

As I watched the day end, I had the feeling that I should lift the blankets covering my grandmother's feet to see if her limbs were dark. If they were then I knew she only had a short time left. I pulled the blankets up and saw that her lower extremities were indeed darkening. She was fading with the day; night was setting in on my grandmother. I had to make a quick decision: did I want to step out of the hospital room to get my mom and my aunt, or did I want to let her peacefully slip away and trust that whoever needed to be there would be? Then the answer came to me: Nanny needed her three girls there: my mom, my aunt, and me. But I didn't want to leave the room. I decided to sit and hold her hand for a few more minutes and say a brief goodbye, in case she left while I was gone. I was still filled with the conviction that Nanny would die holding my hand, that she would never leave me any other way, and that I would comfort her and love her until the end.

As I sat there saying goodbye, someone ran into the room and said, "Renee Wade!" I looked up and the woman quickly realized what she was interrupting and apologized. She explained that she had worked with my grandmother 30 years ago and had seen her name on the door. She thought she was coming in for a reunion. I let her say goodbye to my grandmother. She wondered if there was anything she could do and I asked her to go to the front desk and ask them to call my aunt and tell her it is time. I also asked her to go outside and give my mother the same message. I was grateful that she came to help me. At the same time, to my surprise, Nanny's best friend Sheila called and said she was coming back with her husband to do the rosary. Within minutes, my mother, my aunt, my aunt's husband, Sheila and her husband, and a hospice worker walked into the room. This chaos took a few minutes to get used to and I walked out of the room to prepare for what was about to happen. My prayer was simple: "Let's do this." As I walked back toward the room, a woman hunched over in a wheelchair with obvious signs of dementia looked up at me and asked me the most poignant and existential question of the day.

She simply said, "What are we waiting for?" Exactly! I knew then that the waiting was over. In a few minutes, Nanny would be at peace. I also knew this was not a sad day for my grandmother; it was a day to be celebrated. A homecoming.

I walked back into the room. Sheila and Jim began reciting the rosary. My aunt held one of my grandmother's hands while I held the other. My mom was still too upset to sit down, but she had brought my grandmother's religious music and this created an atmosphere that represented my grandmother perfectly. The first song to come on was, "How Great Thou Art," which Nanny chose to play at her own mother's funeral. This was the most amazing synchronicity, and tears streamed down everyone's cheeks. My mom finally calmed down and sat next to me and we both held my grandmother's hand together. My mom's hand was on top of Nanny's holding it, and mine was underneath it, palm to palm. The music continued and Sheila kept praying in the background. We all blasted Nanny with love, holding her the way she had always held us. It was our turn to be at her bedside, keeping vigil, asking for mercy, trusting in the Lord she prayed to every day. Then the last song finished. Someone went to change the CD and I said, "No, silence now." I knew we didn't have time for another song.

Then, all of a sudden, I was transported out of the hospital room. Anyone else in the room would tell you differently, as I was clearly still there, eyes open, holding Nanny's hand, but the only way I can describe it is that part of me wasn't. I found myself walking in the dark, in the woods, arm in arm with someone. We were climbing steps to reach a well-lit house that shined brightly in the darkness. We could hear the laughter in the distance and as we neared the house, I was filled with anticipation and my heart beat fast. I was walking into a surprise party with the guest of honor and I couldn't wait to get inside. As we opened the door to step out of the cold, I was almost blinded by the light. It was so radiant. I could make out hundreds of people, but I couldn't see their faces as the light was too bright. We were blasted with so much love that I couldn't move forward. All I wanted to do was move closer to that love, that light, that party, and to my Uncle Bobby and Poppy. I couldn't see their faces, but I could feel that they were there in the sea of people. As I tried to cross over the threshold, I was thrown back into the room in the nursing home, at my grandmother's bed side, and I said with pure excitement and joy, "Nanny is about to be the happiest she has ever been." The second I said that, she squeezed my hand and took her last breath.

Nanny let me travel with her, arm in arm, until the bitter end; her final gift to me. She was a mother until the very end. Even on her deathbed, she still found a way to spare me pain, to make the worst thing imaginable the most beautiful and miraculous thing I have ever experienced. On what should have been the worst day of my life, she made me feel such gratitude. She took me the furthest I could possibly go with her, while still remaining here on earth. I literally watched as my grandmother, this great source of light, got absorbed into the light of the world, into the unity of all things. I still see her on a beautiful day at the beach when a hawk flies overhead, when the light on a tugboat moves through the San Francisco fog, when children laugh, when an expecting mother places her hand on her belly. Nanny is there, in all those moments. I see her and feel her and she reminds me that everything around me is a miracle. That she is in all things and that every little thing is Divine.

I left the nursing home that night feeling so much peace and love. It took a few hours for me to soak in the experience and realize what a gift I had been given by my grandmother and by God. When I returned home, I had to write my grandmother's eulogy and make the programs and collages. On the day of the service I was so touched by all of the people who came up to me and told me how she had affected their lives, how she had believed in them and healed them of their physical ailments. Indeed she was a Divine and humble woman. I always thought she was such a simple being, because she was incredibly peaceful and she lived a modest, humble life. But in reality, she was a powerful, magical woman, full of grace.

A few days after the service, I returned to California. One night, someone pointed out that Nanny died on 11/21/11. I knew that, but what I didn't know was that November 21st is the Feast Day of the Presentation of the Virgin Mary. I didn't know what that meant, but I did know that my grandmother had prayed to the Virgin Mary every day. There were pictures of the Virgin Mary hanging all over her house, in her room, and over her bed. In our backyard there was a statue of the Virgin Mary, and one in the bedroom too, so I knew it was significant. I searched online for "The Feast Day of the Presentation of the Virgin Mary." Apparently, this is the day when the Virgin Mary, at the age of 3, was brought to temple by her parents to fulfill her vow as the future mother of Christ. This meant she would remain there for nine years. According to Wikipedia, The Roman Catholic Church refers to this day as "the day we celebrate that dedication of herself, which Mary made to God from her very childhood under the inspiration of the Holy Spirit who filled her with grace." Those words remind me of my grandmother's piety and the way she too dedicated her life to the service of God, and also the grace in which she walked through this world. But what struck me more than these words were the images that appeared before my eyes. The pictures associated with this day are of a woman walking up a long flight of stairs with her daughter, Mary, as they enter a temple to prepare Mary for her sacred vow to become the mother of Jesus. In other words, Mary, the ultimate matriarch, was preparing to meet Jesus and live in God's house—much like Nanny, the ultimate matriarch, was preparing to meet Jesus and live in God's house. The image of the mother and her daughter was strikingly similar to the vision I had experienced by my grandmother's bedside when she took her last breath. Moreover, that very same picture hung above my grandmother's bed when I was growing up. It was a gift from my mother to her mother. To me, it could not be more symbolic or meaningful that my grandmother chose to leave this world on a day associated with the mother of all, because in truth, my grandmother was the mother of all.

February came and by now I was completely at peace with my grandmother's death. It was the most peaceful, wonderful experience of my life, so I didn't worry about her much. I felt that she was living in the light and I was comforted by the thought that she was celebrating at that great party with my uncle and Pop. My uncle's untimely death was devastating to my grandmother and I had no doubt that the reunion with him must have been beautiful. In fact, when she was lying down and reaching up towards heaven, I was certain that it was he who was coming to pull her over. On this one night in February, I went to bed early and fell sound asleep, when I had a dream. I was pushing a door open and I peeked into a room to see Nanny sitting in a chair, peaceful, pain-free, and lucid. Then another door opened and my young uncle, looking healthy and strong, entered the room and walked over to his mother. She said his name with tears in her eyes and joy in her heart. He said, "Mom," and embraced her, kneeled down, and held her hands. She cried soft, happy tears. He held her hand tenderly, comforted her, and they talked softly. Pure love moved between them. I kept peeking into the room, but I couldn't push the door all the way open or enter. Somehow I unconsciously knew that I had just been given another gift: the gift of seeing a mother and her son reunite for the first time. It seemed to be an extension of the vision I had at my grandmother's deathbed. I didn't want to wake from this dream. Once again, I stared into a very bright room feeling the purest, most powerful feeling of love. It was euphoric. But then I suddenly dropped back into my world and opened my eyes to find myself in my bed. Disoriented, I reached for my phone to see what time it was: midnight, and

February 4th had just turned into February 5th. Nanny's birthday was on the 4th and Uncle Bobby's on the 5th.

I have been given so many gifts by this Divine woman. At the end of the speech I gave at her funeral, I explained how if you look at any picture of my grandmother she is literally radiating light onto whomever she is with. She is always looking at one of her children or grandchildren in awe and beaming a healing, loving light on them. To be in my grandmother's presence is to stand in the sunshine. So I told everyone who was mourning her on that day that there was no reason to be sad and that they should only feel gratitude. I closed with the words, "If you were ever lucky enough to stand in the sunshine of Nanny's love, you have been blessed, your soul has been warmed, and there is a piece of her light, her magic, shining inside of you. Tomorrow, I will go home and take this gift of love and light back to California and shine it on my son and my husband, because the gift of light must be given away and shared. As long as we shine our love and light, Nanny is alive, she is with us, and all around us."

Nanny blessed me and taught me to believe in miracles. She taught me to be open and ready to receive love and light and also to give it away. While I watched her die, I held on to those lessons she taught me and saw miracle after miracle unfold. I leave you with these words by the Grateful Dead: "Sometimes you get shown the light in the strangest of places if you look at it right."

With gratitude, I am wishing all of you love and light and the ability to see miracles in everything you do.

MARILYN ST-PIERRE
Psychic and Medium
Hawaii, United States

The night before I was initiated into Kriya Yoga by a yoga master in 1988, I saw a flash of light by the window. I thought there was a storm outside. The following day, I met one of the other people to be initiated and he said he had seen a flash of white light outside his window too. Many years later, before the passing of this master, I took a photo of him and there was white light coming out of him.

Before my Reiki initiation I had another very beautiful experience. The Reiki master was speaking when suddenly the whole room turned into white light and I saw all his chakras lined up in front of his body. I felt as though a high presence of light had entered the room to work with the master, allowing me to have this visual experience. In 2010, I was interviewed to demonstrate my Reiki energy healing. The flash on the photographer's camera broke. He continued to take pictures, then he stopped and said, "Oh, look!"

He had captured a green light coming from my hand as I was administering Reiki energy to the client.

LAUREN NEMETH GONZALEZ
Co-Owner of Greywolf Ministries
Otis, Oregon, United States

One beautiful day when I was 4 years old I ran to my next-door neighbor's home to see my friend. I was known in the neighborhood for pulling up the roses. The look of a rose has always fascinated me. I would take a rose, pull off each petal, and place them in the palm of my hand. Then I would squish them, inhale the amazing fragrance, and throw the petals into the sky, as if thanking the universe for such a gorgeous creation. On this particular day, I decided to take the petals and show my friend.

Amidst all this excitement, we found what we thought were pink wafer candies sitting in a bowl outside the garage door. My friend took them all out and counted them. There were 57 candies, just waiting to be gobbled up! However, unbeknownst to us at the time, they weren't candies; they were rat poison.

I said, "I will eat them first!" They were yummy! I must have eaten over half the bowl, and then my friend was about to take her turn. But all of a sudden I said I did not feel well. I became pale and said that maybe she should not try them, so she did not. My body felt numb and my tummy hurt like I had been kicked in the stomach real hard. I thought I had eaten too much. I walked outside for an hour or so, feeling worse and worse by the minute. My mom thought I was napping on the couch at the time, as she was napping too.

I walked around looking up at the beautiful sky, and passing the rose bushes, all the while becoming increasingly ill. About that time, my dad drove home from work. All I remember from that point was my dad running around in a crazy fit and literally tossing me into our car. Everything was a blur. I felt scared. I remember my dad driving very fast and then I saw light—beautiful white light...the most amazing, calm, and peaceful light I have ever experienced. I found myself looking out into a meadow full of so many flowers. Then I looked up and saw the most beautiful angel! She looked like Mother Mary. She bowed down to me and said, "You are a gentle, pure soul. You will go back now as you have much to do." She smiled and kissed me on the cheek. When she left there was a beautiful white light and complete peace—a calm that I still remember to this day, when I feel stressed.

This experience is the basis of all I have challenged myself to become, seeking deep within my soul. The next thing I remember is being pulled from this amazing white light to see doctors all around me. I felt the most nauseating and excruciating, dizzy pain in my stomach and head. I was told I had to have vitamin K shots into my stomach. The next thing I knew I threw up every ounce of those "candies" straight onto the doctor. I cried, but he said that he was glad I had thrown up on him, and that everything would be okay. They kept me in this sterile, frightening place for a day.

In my hometown I was called "the miracle girl" because the newspaper said I ate enough poison to kill 10 horses. It was not my time to go. When I returned home, I cried, feeling afraid because I had seen my truths, and at that age I did not understand what I saw and felt. I have never forgotten this experience. It molded me for my future life happenings. I spent the next 48 years searching for answers, affirmations, and truths about life, death, purity, clarity, and love.

Then, two years ago, in 2012, I had another Divine awakening experience, born out of all my life's trials and tribulations. It was like a great landslide of love and light that took me to my darkest places. But I crawled up to the light, both visually and spiritually. It was truly the most memorable and remarkable moment in my life. The spirits and angel guides heard my cries, and in a moment of complete awakening, everything that is Me came forward to the present. It was a simple, yet profound moment, and it took everything in me to accept love. Now just writing the word *love* makes me sing, knowing that our angels are here and always have been.

I attended a special ceremony, and met an amazing soul. This man saw my pain, and my purity. In the midst of this gathering, he came and sat with me, and asked, "May I give this gift to you?" He opened my hands and placed a single white eagle feather in my palms. I held it graciously with my palm open. He then began to talk. We laughed and smiled. By accident, his leg touched mine. At that moment my life transformed. My head became light and a pure white beam of light shot straight up to the heavens. Divine purpose was revealed to me in an instant. I felt overwhelmed, but I was not afraid. In this moment, I saw. I heard. Unbeknownst to him and me, he was not speaking with his tongue, but with his mind and soul. Something changed deep within me. I had experienced Divinity at its greatest. Then I sat, and tears rolled down my cheeks; happy, beautiful tears.

This man brought me the most amazing and divine gift, as I am now able to love openly and freely, unconditionally. In my deepest meditation and prayer, which is a gift to oneself, I love my family, friends, and of course my soul mate. I have grown so much since realizing and believing in love. I have learned that love can take us anywhere. I have been transformed. So I take this grand love and extend it to those in need, to those who want to "see," and to those who need a smile. Everything falls into place as it is meant to. With my positivity and self love, all has been revealed to me. I am so humbly grateful for my life experiences, and to the beautiful angel who came to me at 4 years old, to give me the divine gifts of Love and Light.

DAVID DINNER
Writer
Kilauea, Hawaii, United States

I went to the meditation evening in San Francisco for one simple reason: to sleep with the yogini who had invited me! She had the face of a celebrity, with straight, pearly teeth, and curly blonde California hair. She had begged me to come with her, even if she did make it clear that we would be in separate rooms! Over the previous months, I had taken a few of her yoga classes and finally, probably to stop me from drooling on her feet, she agreed to meet me for lunch and a glass of wine. Over the dregs of Zinfandel she gave me a complimentary palm reading, and when she gazed at my hand, a look of pleasant surprise crossed her face, which she quickly masked. Then, with what felt like carefully chosen words, she said, "David, you have special skills you have not yet discovered. Come to the Intensive in the city. I know you're supposed to go. Please, say yes."

Three thousand people sat in quiet anticipation of the arrival of the famous spiritual teacher. My head was overflowing with chatter: "I'm not devoid of awareness. After all, I've had at least 10 years of personal growth courses and know my way around the hotbeds of the New Age, the Bay Area, and the Esalen Institute in Big Sur. I've even gone through the Reiki Master program and have added energy healing to my dental practice. I'm finding a measure of success treating my patients with energy work, but I have many friends who seem far more advanced than I. They are able to see the auras of their clients. I want to learn how to do that. There's no chance that this woman can show me the way. That's for me to develop on my own, isn't it? I don't need a guru to fix me. I know all too well that I am far from perfect. The parade of women who march through my so-called love life make that abundantly clear."

With all that in my head, I sat there, ready to flee the event, barely realizing that the chatter in the back of my brain was always there.

However, when the woman dressed in red silk entered the auditorium, everything changed. I felt a rolling vibration as she came through the doorway behind me. As she moved down the center aisle, everyone held their breath and the hair on my neck stood on end as if something momentous was happening. I dismissed it, telling myself it was just a draft, but somewhere in the depths of my heart there was a stirring, a wishing for something I did not possess, an end to the tunnel of emptiness I had drifted through for so many years.

Now at the front of the room, her voice came out with a warm smile. "Take a comfortable upright posture with your sitting bones in contact with your seat. You can fold your hands in your lap or place them in chin mudra." She demonstrated the position with the thumbs touching the index fingers, resting palms down on the legs. I had the strangest feeling that when she spoke, she was addressing her words to me alone; that, mysteriously, she knew I was there, despite the fact that we had never met. Even from a distance, her eyes burned into mine. I would not have been too shocked if she called out to me by name. I had never felt so "seen."

"Now, without effort, allow your breath to lengthen and silently repeat the mantra, Om Namah Shivayah."

My mind raced with resistance, coming up with a hundred reasons why I should escape, leave now while I still could.

She continued, "Imagine the Light of ten thousand suns above your head. Now bring the Light down into your head and then into your mouth. Om Nama Shivayah."

I could see the Light. I could even feel it. Then my awareness drifted and I began to lose myself. "Om Nama Shivayah." It was like swimming into a mysterious cave. The room seemed to darken and I felt myself sliding into the darkness. Then there was nothing. I was unaware of my whereabouts and I felt my mind somewhere on the surface, thinking random, disconnected snippets of nothingness, while Om Nama Shivayah continued cycling through me. After a long while, I noticed a bright golden pinpoint of light in the darkness and I thought, "That is not the light of ten thousand suns. It is too small." The light hung in space somewhere in the distance, then slowly moved toward me in an arc, picking up speed until it struck me between my eyes. My entire being illuminated with an unbounded feeling I had never known, but I sensed it must be joy.

From somewhere...inside of me or outside, everywhere or nowhere...wordless words shivered through me: "You will see."

A curtain had dropped and everything changed. The cryptic message defied exact interpretation. "You will see" could mean so many things. Of course I wondered *what* it was I would see. Or *why*. But in the end, I let it go and decided to wait to find out. Nevertheless, there was one thing in the message I did not have to wait for. One thing was clear: for the first time in my direct experience, I felt certain that there was something beyond me, guiding me, protecting me. For the first time in my experience, I felt safe.

ROISHEEN KEATING
Retired Childminder
Torre del Mar, Spain

Around 24 hours after I attended a Shamanic healing ritual, I was lying in bed when I heard a noise in my ears. I didn't want to open my eyes, so I ignored it, but after the third time of hearing it, I decided to open my eyes after all. Despite the darkness I could see a man sitting on the side of the bed with his back to me. At first I thought it was my husband, but I could feel *him* sleeping next to me, like he did every night. The man seemed real and he was dressed in a blue jumper, but I couldn't see his face. After a while he faded away. I then looked up at the ceiling above my head and I saw five faces looking down at me. They were see-through and joined together at the edges. One seemed to be an old lady and another had only one eye in the middle of its forehead. They were all happy looking. I didn't recognize any of them and I didn't dare to move in case I disturbed them. I was completely transfixed, and then, shortly after, they faded away.

I live on the 10th floor of an apartment block with security blinds on the windows, so no light enters my bedroom. Nevertheless, in the middle of the night, during the winter, I woke up and my entire bedroom was bathed in light. I glanced around, bewildered, and noticed dark shadows of palm trees on the walls and ceiling. It felt like I was in the middle of a forest. I stared at these images, momentarily amazed, and then woke my husband up to ask if he could see them too. He confirmed that he could. Soon after that they faded away. Since then we have woken many times in the night to see patterns of light, and shapes, such as circles, stars, and flowers against the dark background.

RAEDERLE PHOENIX LYDELL WEST JACOT
Nutritional Consultant
Lihue, Hawaii, United States

"I've never seen light like this," he whispered. "It's so beautiful."

One night at a Christmas house party I had drunk a little alcohol. I didn't like the taste much. However, I did like the subtle swaying feeling generally referred to as "being tipsy."

The party started late and went on into the early hours of the morning. After several hours I was tired of socializing, sipping alcoholic beverages, and awaiting the *zing* that made the evening fun. I had brought a man called Justin with me, and we were both tired and ready to leave, but the third person we came with wanted to stay until the party ended.

I had a hunch that meditation would sooth my troubled nerves and I suggested this to Justin. He liked the idea so we found a quiet room and entered without bothering to turn on the lights. Anyone who may have seen us enter the room probably assumed we were seeking privacy for a different reason!

I had grown up with regular meditation circles held at home, so I knew a little about how to meditate. First you relax. Then you turn off the lights and make the room as dark as possible. Then you get comfortable, generally with the back straight and the palms facing upwards. And then you ask for protection.

In my mind's eye I formed a white screen around me that only let good energy flow through. Funneling in through the top streamed the white light of Christ and the light surrounded me, filled me, and protected me.

I am in the infinite light and the infinite light is within me.

I don't recall what I said for a "lead in" all those years ago. At that stage I hadn't practiced leading meditation. I recall prompting

Justin to tell me what he could see. We were sitting cross-legged across from one another, our knees not quite touching.

"It is dark," he said. "And cold."

I prompted him to continue.

"I am trapped. Black walls are closing in on me from every direction!" His voice was filled with fear. I had never heard someone so afraid. I asked him to come out and wake up, but he would not. I guessed that I could turn on the lights and shake him out of it, but something inside me said, *that is not the way.*

Soundlessly I moved my upward-facing palms side by side a few inches above my lap. In my palms I envisioned a miniature Jesus about 10 inches tall: the stereotypical Jesus with the flowing white linen robes, the golden hair, and the tanned skin.

My vision was simply a focal point where I built more and more white light. I let this vision grow brighter and bolder as Justin whimpered a foot or so away from me. I didn't touch him or move anything apart from my hands. Gesturing a few inches forward with my palms I sent the Christ Light into his chest. I'm not sure what I expected to happen, but I was quite startled by his immediate response. He gasped and said, "It's so bright!" His voice was filled with awe and tears. "I've never seen light like this," he whispered. "It's beautiful."

Justin exhaled loudly as though he had been holding his breath, and in the dark room I might have seen the tension leave his body or I might have sensed it. With my mind I had freed him from his darkness, like an ancient Egyptian priest, like a practiced monk, like a true Reiki practitioner. That night, it was no longer a theory that I could heal with light, but a fact.

I have seen many small miracles in my life, but all of them lend validity to the truth and power of light.

Chapter 2:
Spiritual Awakenings

*I*t's not unusual for people to experience sudden spiritual awakenings at the most bizarre times of their life. Without rhyme or reason, someone's life path can seem to transform in front of their eyes with no explanation or warning. That's what happened to Cynthia Segal in her story (on page 48), but my own awakening happened in a very different way.

First, I endured a life-stopping spell of depression.

Unexpectedly, I was quite literally plunged into the dark in order to finally see the Light, and awaken from my "sleep." Often I would curl up on my sofa for hours on end and do nothing but cry, wail, and sob, until all that emotion passed out of my system. Hours later, for no apparent reason, the crying would resume, stronger and louder than before. The days blended into nights, and nights seemed to last forever, as tears streamed down my cheeks into the early hours. I no longer knew who I was, or what I was here on planet Earth for. At times, I even had suicidal thoughts, thinking I'd be better off dead than here for no reason, watching my life whittle away in front of my eyes and feeling useless. Desperate to know my life purpose and sure that I was here to achieve something not only unique, but also great, I battled through every day sullen, miserable, and enormously frustrated.

When I reached my lowest point, I looked up and asked God for a sign. He responded in less than 24 hours. I found the answer in the pages of a magazine, which led me to meet a man named Richard Waterborn who did cellular healing sessions. His incredible work helped me to release old stagnant energy in my cells that had been trapped due to a traumatic incident when I was 17 years old. Other energies were also dealt with, including those stemming from past lives. This marked a remarkable transformation in my life and I began to see situations and people in a whole new Light. One day as I strolled along the beach promenade—the same promenade I had strolled dozens of times before—I stopped at the foot of a tree and gazed at it in awe for several minutes. I began to see beauty in everything and everyone. This enabled me to also see the beauty in myself, perhaps for the first time ever, and as a result life became a magical adventure, full of countless synchronicities and miracles. That's when I started seeing spirit too.

Maybe your own awakening has already occurred. If not, then by opening your mind and believing, through reading the true-life stories in this section, I'd hazard a guess that your awakening will happen very soon! It's time to rejoice and bathe in the joy, peace, and love that are constantly present in our lives—which we didn't see or acknowledge before!

DINA PROCTOR

Best-selling Author of **Madly Chasing Peace: How I Went from Hell to Happy in Nine Minutes a Day**
Los Angeles, California, United States

Five years ago I didn't want to live anymore. I felt like I had a gaping black hole inside of myself that, no matter what I tried, I couldn't fill. I was clinically depressed, hopelessly addicted to alcohol (and food, and money, and men), and had tried to fix myself in uncountable ways over the previous 10 years, starting with moving from the East Coast to the West just after college.

At first I thought I just needed to move away from what was known and comfortable—*A new city, a fresh start,* I thought. So I moved from where I grew up on Long Island, New York, to southern California. I also thought that maybe helping people would help me to "find myself" so I signed up for a full-time volunteer position at a homeless shelter. I settled in, eager to give of myself in order to feel the elusive satisfaction of deep joy and personal fulfillment. To feel as though my life meant something. To feel as though I was a good person, doing good in the world.

However, after a few months at the shelter, I couldn't help but notice that this black hole inside of me was not shrinking. In fact, I felt like it was getting bigger. *Maybe I wasn't helping enough people?* I knew the solution—more volunteering outside of my work hours.

I signed up to tutor kids in the evenings at a family shelter. I spent hours re-immersing myself in everything from geometry homework to basic reading skills. *A kid in need? I'm here to help!* That was my motto. And after my tutoring hours were complete I joined folks driving around town to all the bakeries in the late-night hours to pick up the leftover bread and food to serve to homeless folks at yet another shelter. My weekends were filled with cooking gigantic vats of soup and making hundreds of sandwiches to feed to the people living in the local park. Every spare minute I had was devoted to helping another in need.

I knew the work I was doing was good work. I was greatly appreciated by those with whom I volunteered, and by the homeless people with whom I was forming relationships. Everything looked as though it should be contributing toward my own inner satisfaction and happiness. I was following the right formula, after all—help others and you will help yourself!

So why did I still feel like my inner emptiness was growing?

The answer eluded me for several more years, which I devoted to helping people in Third World countries. (*Maybe the homeless people I was working with just weren't* poor *enough*, I thought—*I needed to travel abroad!*) I went to Africa and stayed in places without running water or electricity. I went to Guatemala and helped improve school programs. These were the neediest people and I was helping them! I was also living very simply with no material attachments. Finally, I'd found it. The key to happiness.

Except that it wasn't.

My inner desperation continued to grow, and finally I sought out a therapist through my health insurance. She suggested that I join a clinical depression support group. This group met three times a week, during my working hours. But that was no problem—my doctor granted me medical leave from my nonprofit job at the time and I attended every session.

It gave me some relief to realize I wasn't the only person suffering from this inescapable, all-consuming emotional black hole inside of myself, but after a few weeks of complaining, crying, and commiserating with my new friends, I dropped out of the program. I felt as though it was dragging me down even further, being surrounded by other unhappy people. So my therapist suggested something new: medication. That, I knew, would fix me! *Some good strong drugs to even out my chemical imbalance and I'll be good to go.* The window of hope opened a little and I was able to breathe in some proverbial fresh air. But then I wondered, *What would it really look like to be happy?*

I'd never known what it was like to be happy. Even as a kid I was a perfectionist, a quiet kid who tried to achieve straight As and be the best in the class. I was never abused as a child—nothing was terribly abnormal about my childhood—and yet I had been uptight, anxious, and dissatisfied from as far back as I could remember. That inner emptiness had grown and expanded over the years.

But this medication idea might work. I was looking forward to getting started on it. So I started my first antidepressant protocol. To my disappointment all the pills did for me was make me want to sleep. All of the time—for hours and hours during the day, and hours and hours at night. I was constantly groggy and numb. And frustrated that this wasn't the big cure I'd been hoping for after all.

Since that first medication didn't work, I tried a different one, then another and another. I even ended up in a research study program and participated in a clinical experimental medication. These pills made me feel nauseous. I constantly had to pull the car over to the side of the road while I was driving and hang up in mid-conversation during phone calls so I could go and throw up.

Another failure at fixing myself checked off the list.

While all of this experimentation was going on I was also changing everything about my environment to see if those were the factors depressing me. I moved apartments. I changed cities. I upgraded my boyfriends. I bought newer and better cars. I went on diets, I tried cleanses, I went off sugar, I went back on sugar, I gave up meat, I ate meat, I went high-protein, I went high-carb. You name it, I tried it.

And the self-help books. Oh, the self-help books! My shelves were lined with them. I would read a little of each one as I got them, but never had the motivation to immerse myself in their get-happy-quick tips, so nothing ever changed. The thermometer on my emotional life was stuck at the level of: Horribly Depressed and Sick of Trying to Fix Myself.

After almost 10 years of all of this work, the incessant changes, the medications, the cleanses, the jobs, the boyfriends, the cars, I finally discovered something that really worked. Something that made me feel better than almost anything. That gave me confidence I'd never felt before. That made me feel attractive, funny, cute, and *wonderful*.

Alcohol.

Alcohol had always been in the background for me. I'd never been drawn to it, until I reached such desperation inside myself that it became immensely appealing. In a relatively short amount of time I went from partying on weekends (with yet another set of roommates in yet another new place to live) to partying six nights a week, to drinking in the mornings to ward off hangovers, to drinking all day long—at work, at home: anywhere and everywhere. Just give me my vodka and all would be well.

Until it wasn't.

For those of you who may be wondering how this sad tale made its way into a book about Awakening and Light, don't worry, that part is coming.

As my drinking increased my concern about the moral fiber of my character decreased. I was becoming someone I didn't recognize. I was stealing money, lying to my friends, using men I'd just met, and the list goes on. I reached a point after more than two years of constant alcohol in my bloodstream where I could no longer live with who I had become. And that's the day I decided to make a plan to take my own life.

One Sunday evening in the fall of 2008 I decided that that following Saturday I would end it. I'd give myself that week to get everything together at home and at work before I left this world for good. Put myself out of my misery. Not because I wanted to die, but because I had tried everything I could think of to make me want to live and nothing was working. I hated myself, my life, and just about everything about just about everything. It was time to hit the Power Off button.

But on that Sunday night I was in such emotional agony that I didn't think I could make it even six more days to fulfill my plan. I needed to feel better, to make it one more week, but how? Then an idea occurred to me: *It might make me feel better to see how bad it might have been—to see what lives that were worse than mine looked like.* I was living down the street from an addiction recovery center and thought if I could anonymously go and get a glimpse of some of those folks I might feel better about myself, my drinking, and who I had become.

So I went. They had open meetings for the community to join so I sat in the very back row and listened to the people speaking at the front of the room, telling their stories. And then, completely unexpectedly, I began crying.

Denial is very common among those of us (currently or previously) in the throes of addiction. And what was coming as a complete surprise to me was the realization that my life was *worse* than some of the stories I was hearing. *Only one bottle of wine a night? Please. Stopping to get help before you started stealing and waking up next to people you had only known for three hours? Really. How on earth is it that you are here telling your story yet I don't think I belong here?*

This realization was the beginning of my awakening. And those tears were the very, very tender beginning of my own healing.

The women in that room completely took me by surprise—they didn't even ask my name but sat next to me while tears streamed endlessly down my face, holding my hands, and gently brushing my tangled hair away from my face. I'd never ever known such compassion from complete strangers. Their human touches were some of the most meaningful I'd ever experienced. Without exchanging words I knew they had been where I was, and that they knew the secret of how to dig themselves out before suicide became the only option.

I stuck around the program because it felt good to be there, but I didn't commit to living by its teachings (or quitting drinking for that matter) for almost three months. I was too busy postponing my suicide one day at a time. I kept telling myself, *You don't have to kill yourself today; you can always do it tomorrow.* The people at the recovery center focused on not drinking one day at a time. I focused on staying a member of the human population one day at a time.

Then one day at the meeting I went to I hear a certain woman speak. I'll call her Grace, because that is exactly what she exuded, and that is (eventually) exactly what she became to me: my saving Grace. She sat in front of this big room of more than 50 people in her designer skinny jeans and with her cute little haircut, all put together and perfect, talking about how her heroin addiction had led her down more horrific paths than alcohol had taken me.

I could not believe that the woman she was describing was the same woman telling this story—she was so pretty and confident and warm and honest. I was so drawn to her that I went up to her after the meeting and asked for her phone number. We met for coffee and she told me how she did it—how she climbed out of hell and into an amazing life she had never known was possible. I told her I wanted that too, and she said she would help me, talk to me every single day, and teach me the way.

Grace was a tough-love kind of mentor. She didn't fall for any of my sweet talk or excuses. She would tell me, "If you want what I have, you have to do the work." And it turned out the first of this "work" was to learn to meditate. *What? I rebelled. Meditate? What exactly does that mean? And more importantly, how on earth is sitting there in a floaty, wistful way going to help with any of this self-hatred and suicidal obsession I'm stuck in? And how will that take away this intense physical and emotional compulsion to drink constantly?* I balked at her suggestion. But she seemed to expect that. Grace's response to me was, "If your way was working you wouldn't be here with me right now, you'd be off living your life happily ever after. But here you are, so why don't you try my way for a while?"

That was a good point. I agreed to try it her way.

Grace's first meditation instruction was to sit still every morning and focus on my breathing for 20 minutes. *How hard could that be?* I agreed to give it a try.

The first morning I set a timer and settled in for my 20 minutes. But after about 30 seconds the craving to drink overwhelmed me, and negative thoughts about suicide and self-hatred flared up strongly. I forced myself to endure the inner agony and sit as still as I could, as I focused on my breathing. But after only about three minutes, my skin was crawling, I was shaking and sweating uncontrollably, and I physically could not sit still any longer. So I got up, cried a little, and slowly, painfully went about my day.

A couple of hours later it nagged at me that I hadn't completed the entire 20 minutes as Grace had instructed. So I tried to sit down again, setting the timer, and using all of my effort to try and focus on my breathing. Predictably, after about three minutes the experience again became intolerable and I ended the meditation.

Day after day this went on. Three minutes here, three minutes there. Three minutes was my limit. I thought Grace would be disappointed in my failure to follow her directions, but she was surprisingly encouraging, telling me whatever I was capable of doing was great.

After about eight weeks of this messy three-minutes-at-a-time meditation practice, something unexpected happened. I came out of my three-minute meditation and even though I was in my same old apartment, nothing about it was "same old" to me. I opened my eyes and looked around the room, noticing my everyday things as if for the first time. They had a special glow about them: the wooden furniture, the candles, and especially my cat. My vision was different; I felt like I had switched into a 3D-movie way of seeing the world. And when I got up from my seated meditation I noticed that my conscious awareness was several feet above and slightly behind my body. I was acutely aware that this higher vantage point was actually where the "real" me was all the time—above my physical self, always present but never accessed.

How could I have never known this? That these physical bodies are like little finger puppets we animate to navigate the physical world, but that our true essence, the "puppeteer," is actually much, much bigger than our small bodies?

I stayed in this state of hovering above my body for about three days. For this entire time period I had absolutely no mind chatter. I had never even known that was possible! I had no negative thoughts. Not a single one. And I fell in love with everyone I met—not in "love" like I did with guys when I was drunk at bars, but true, honest, real appreciation and connection with every single person's soul essence. I became capable of extended eye contact and long silences. I saw the personalities of trees and flowers (*who knew? They have souls and intentions too!*), the innermost essence of love within and throughout every single living being.

From this state it was plain to me that anything I wanted in the physical world could be found by focusing on it from this larger, higher state of being. That the physical world is merely a mirror, a reflection, of the depth of the connection between the "little me" (my physical self) and the "big me" (my soul-essence Self). Knowing this connection exists and keeping it prominent in my life became my number-one priority.

And then my life started to evolve big time.

I stayed with Grace through the recovery program. I made amends for stealing, repaired relationships with people I'd hurt, completely revamped my close relationships, healed from addiction, and lost the weight I'd gained after my drinking addiction became an eating addiction. Every single thing I wanted to do I found in my three-minute meditations first.

I became happier and happier in my life. I had never even known this state of deep happiness was possible when I was a drunken disaster. My best high from those times was a million times less satisfying than the bad days I experienced after learning how to connect with my higher self. Alcohol, men, money, food—all of my old demons lost their appeal.

I learned that I'd been seeking empowerment all those years—the true connection to my inner source of power, peace, and wisdom. I'd been plugging into all of these other things, seeking satisfaction, but they never quite fit right and I'd always needed more and more (and more). But this higher-self connection was amazingly and deeply fulfilling in a way I'd never experienced.

Those three days, my work with Grace, and my willingness to face my demons and heal, changed—and saved—my life.

Today, I use my peace to help other people find theirs. I teach what I call 3x3 Meditation—three minutes, three times a day. I love speaking to groups, working with people one on one, and co-creating with people who are experts in wellness methods, to share the message that no matter where you are, what you've done, or who you think you've become, you can always, *always* get back to the Light.

CYNTHIA SEGAL

Intuitive and Psychic
Hollywood, Florida, United States

One afternoon, I was sitting there minding my own business when the phone rang.

"Cynthia? Can you help me?"

"Of course, Annette, what's wrong?"

"I can't find my car keys and I need to take my dad to the hospital!"

"Okay, I'll drive right over!"

"No, no, just help me calm down, and then I'll be able to find them."

"Okay."

We talked for a while, and then suddenly I saw her car keys in an image that appeared in my head!

"Annette?" I said.

"Yes?"

"I think I see your car keys on a white table behind some books!"

"Well they can't be on the white table because... Oh my God, Cynthia! They fell behind the books! How did you know that?"

"I don't know. A picture popped into my head."

"Really? Okay, bye. I love you."

"Bye, Annette. I love you too. Drive carefully."

What was that? I thought. *What just happened? How did I get that picture of Annette's keys, and how was it so clear?*

Throughout the next few hours I received every psychic skill I had ever heard of or read about—and probably some I still haven't discovered. I remember having a conversation with God, whom I thought I had always been talking to, but this was different. I said to Him, "Please don't get me wrong, this is an amazing skill set, but I think you meant to give this to my neighbor? She's already into all of this woo-woo stuff. She loves crystals and candles, but I'm just an unhappy computer geek, and sorry but I don't really believe in all of this." At that moment I heard and felt laughter in my head, immediately followed by the feeling of an inner hug, whereby every cell in my body relaxed. It was the most wonderful thing I have ever experienced.

That moment, after 30 years of working with computer systems, was the beginning of my journey. I am now ranked in the world's top 20 intuitives, as the "Best and Most Trusted Psychic and Healer."

My life had been pretty black-and-white until that moment. I was not fond of my work, my colleagues, my environment, or the way I felt all day.

A gentleman I met on a plane once asked me, "How did you become a psychic? Were you that way from birth?" When I told him my story, he answered with, "Not strong enough! You need something that jumps out...multiple heart attacks, or maybe you died twice and came back!"

I laughed.

"Yes," I said, "I guess those stories are more exciting, but I think I'll go with the truth."

KIMBERLEY JONES
Intuitive Mentor for Awakening Women
Devon, United Kingdom

Fifteen years ago, before waking up to what was really going on beneath the surface, before my sudden and intense spiritual awakening that changed everything, I was trying to keep it together. I was 25 years old and had left home after university to live alone in a new apartment. I had a new job and a new boyfriend, and I thought I was pretty happy with my lot. I was putting on a brave face—and self-medicating with tobacco and alcohol. I kept myself busy, tried to be the best caregiver I could possibly be for my mum, who had been ill for more than 10 years, at the same time as playing the role of Agony Aunt for all of my friends. Why? Because if I stopped for one minute and felt what was really going on inside, watching my mother fight for her life every day, seeing her lose parts of her body, her hair, and her dignity, the pain would have been unimaginable. On some level I knew that, so it was easier to have a drink and wear a smile. That is, until life—or rather death—shook me awake, broke me open, tore me limb from limb, chewed me up, and spat out the pieces. No more hiding my true pain. No more pretending. The game was up. Mum died.

My reconnection with the Light came via my parents, but in very different ways. There is a lineage of female psychic seers behind me. Rich in sensitivity and awareness, I grew up watching this lineage as my great-grandmother taught my mother how to read the deeper levels of life. I went to bed at night as a child hearing the excited squeals of my mum's friends as she read their cards or held a séance. Some of my first drawings were of the spirits that showed up in my bedroom. It frightened me a bit, to be honest.

My father's side of the family were devoted Christians. The first whiff they caught of me having "special abilities" caused me to be whisked away to be dunked in the font. I had a hurried Christening at the age of 5. Mum had managed to hold strong until then, defending my right to choose my own spiritual path when I was old enough. But now the thought of me chatting to ancestors in my bedroom was too much, and so I went to church.

I loved it. I loved the peace. I loved the towering stone pillars and sparkling stained glass. But most of all, I felt the love, I sensed the Light, and I felt safe.

There was violence at home and energies I didn't feel comfortable with. At church I escaped all of that and felt bathed in a loving energy. I'm not talking about religion or doctrine or even the church services; I am talking about the pure essence and energy I felt when standing in that beautiful building. That's when I first connected to something that ignited inside. I didn't know what that was at the age of 5; I just knew it felt like home. That was my first experience of the Light.

Over the years I observed my mother's intuitive skills. She had a small hairdressing business that she ran from home. I would help out sometimes; it was fascinating to see her serving people as she put their hair in curlers. She offered deep listening and intuitive, heartfelt guidance to anyone who sat in that wooden chair in the middle of the kitchen floor. They could tell her anything and she would listen. She offered no judgment, only love, plus a dosage of down-to-earth humor.

Every now and then someone would book the last appointment in the diary. We all knew what that meant. I would make a pot of English tea with loose leaves and I'd pour the tea using no strainer. Then, when the client had finished her tea (and picked the odd tea leaf out of her teeth), Mum would swirl it this way and that a certain number of times, pour the last dregs of tea out onto the saucer, and then read the leaves left in the cup.

I picked up skills along the way, but I'd always known things about people, energy, and life, and I wasn't interested in learning more about that. I didn't realize my gifts were anything special, and I was more interested in going out with my friends to let off steam. My childhood years had been filled with fear—my father is a troubled character and it was a relief when my parents divorced. Soon after the end of that long, painful divorce, Mum was diagnosed with breast cancer.

I always had a sense that I was being given a space of Grace when I was younger. An inner knowing told me, "Have fun now, be young, wild, and free; make the most of it. Don't be so serious.

You have great responsibility ahead of you; there will be plenty of time for seriousness later."

So, after a wild time at university, I moved out of the family home, got a job at an art gallery, and moved into a lovely apartment overlooking the sea with my then-boyfriend. Everything was coming together and ticking along nicely, until one day at work I got the call. Mum was dying. She may only have a few hours left to live. The next few hours were a blur. My younger brother collected me from work. I remember shouting, "Oh my God!" over and over again as my mind struggled to absorb was happening.

That weekend the house was full of people. Each person took it in turns to sit with Mum, honoring her and saying their goodbyes. We all wrote cards and letters, brought gifts to her room, and set up a sound system to play meditative music. As it was Christmas we placed a small illuminated Christmas tree at the foot of her bed. It was both harrowing and intensely beautiful.

I took another turn to be with Mum, holding her, laying with her, saying whatever needed saying for me and for her. It was clear that she was getting weaker. Even though hours had turned into a couple of days I knew she was crossing over and I sensed she was holding on so everyone could say goodbye. As I sat with her, I entered a trance-like state. I found myself in another reality walking with Mum hand in hand towards a bright light. All around us was this pink energy and I could feel immense love pulling us towards this light—a cliché, I know, but there was no tunnel, just the sense of a threshold and loved ones beyond it reaching out to Mum. As we approached this "doorway" I felt so compelled to go into that light with her, and I did a little, enough to receive knowledge about what was there, but then I was pushed back with a clear and resounding "no!" With that I snapped back into the room and looked at Mum, who was still with us, but only barely. Relatives came to me insisting I get some sleep. A short while later Mum was gone.

Anyone who has lost someone they love will understand the strange slow-motion reality that takes hold in those first moments of shock as everyone holds their breath. And then the feeling comes. From within came a sound I had never made before and have never made since: a primal cry. I wanted the world to stop. I wanted the world to know that this beautiful, brave, and magnificent woman had passed.

That night I felt compelled to go to the beach. Mum had loved the sea and I felt called there. As I sat looking at the waves and the stars I felt a surge of something startling. I could feel my mother's presence everywhere. It was so strong. What had made her unique was now in the pebbles, the water, the stone step I was sitting on, and the wooden beach huts behind me. She was everywhere, and I could feel her. I could even feel her in the air I was breathing, and there was a strange sense of euphoria. She was free. I could feel her ecstatic release. She was free of pain, and free of her body.

That moment marked the beginning of the transformation of my consciousness. My connection with her was so strong that I experienced what she was experiencing as pure consciousness, free from the bounds of the physical dimension. I got a glimpse of the afterlife process and the continuity of consciousness. But that was just the beginning. Two months after Mum died, I was lying in bed crying. I cried every morning when I awoke, remembering all over again that she had gone. This morning my body was getting warmer and sounds were getting louder. Then I smelled my mum's perfume and it broke my heart wide open. I surged with emotion and grew really hot so I moved to kick the bedding off me to cool down. I found I couldn't move and I couldn't open my eyes. I panicked.

A deafening screeching sound surged through my body as it went into what felt like the worst muscle cramp of my life. I fought it, which probably didn't help, but I felt terrified and tried to shake my body free. My body spasmed violently and a bright light filled me. I felt an immense love, and at the same time I felt like I was dying. Then it ended with a gentle and graceful sigh. I went into meltdown. What had happened to me? I was crying, freaked out, and terrified. I knew my life would never be the same again.

In the months that followed I realized I had received a huge download of abilities and potential from my female lineage of seers. Each day I awoke with a new enhanced sense or level of intuitive awareness. The first experience was my body moving into spontaneous yoga postures. I didn't know what these were at the time. I just learned to go with it because it was painful if I fought against it. Then I saw colors and energy around people, and could read their thoughts and feelings with alarming accuracy. I realized that people think *a lot*. I saw the energy fields and webs running through inanimate objects, and would know each day who was planning to call or visit me. I felt the life force of animals, plants, and trees, and the immense love from nature. When I closed my eyes I saw into the cosmos. My face would change into many faces when I looked in the mirror, and others with intuitive awareness also saw my face change.

Each night further surges of light passed through my body, along with extraordinary experiences. Instead of dreams I saw high-speed slide shows of images from all of human history, science, mathematics, geometry, ancient symbology, and sacred texts. It felt like I was receiving fast-track training in the evolution of human consciousness and the nature of reality.

In time all of this settled, but I had changed. Throughout the "downloads" I always had a clear and reassuring sense that this was a spiritual process and that I was safe. I never lost my center or inner witness. My ego and personality were dissolving, but my inner Self both experienced and observed what was unfolding from safe ground.

Depression and illness followed as the shock and trauma reached my body, and my transformation continued on other levels. It took several years before I realized that what I had been through is referred to as a Spiritual Crisis, Spiritual Emergency, Kundalini Awakening, or Shamanic Initiation.

The process of seeking to make sense of and recover from that first awakening is what landed me on a conscious spiritual path. I chose to learn Reiki, and it was transformational. I was filled with peace and what had felt like recovery slowly became a path of growth. I went on to become a Reiki Master and learned about energy, healing, and consciousness. I studied with spiritual teachers, developed my abilities and gifts, and dedicated myself to daily inner work. I did whatever I could to support my ever-unfolding awakening.

My life is now dedicated to the service of unfolding consciousness and to helping others have a graceful awakening. Sharing my own journey transparently is part of how I do that. I am truly blessed.

GAIL LYNNE GOODWIN
Founder of InspireMeToday.com
Whitefish, Montana, United States

I moved to Los Angeles with my infant daughter when I was 23. I had been there about three years and had just remarried when an extraordinary experience gave me an insight into how the Universe works and how we are all powerful creators.

I was at a point in my life where I was searching for what else is out there, trying to determine who I was and what I wanted to be. I desired to know how the God I grew up with and the spirituality I found in my heart would come together, and how this could be applied, in a practical way, to my life.

In 1987 the Harmonic Convergence took place, a time and date when the planets and stars aligned, allowing energies to flow in a powerful way for the first time in thousands of years, not to occur again until thousands of years in the future. Essentially, it was a celebration. By chance, I met a guy called Jose, whose spiritual name was Sat Nam Singh, which meant "an enlightened teacher" in Hindi. He was a maintenance man at one of the apartment complexes I managed and he told me he was going to Mount Shasta to celebrate the Harmonic Convergence. He said that any spiritual or enlightened seekers were welcome to join him. Intrigued, I went to Mount Shasta in North California with Sat Nam Singh, and brought two of my close friends, Patricia and Daniel.

On the day of the Harmonic Convergence we went hiking early that morning to the top of the north side of Mount Shasta. We started out early, making sure to bring our canteens of water and hiking shoes. Northern California in the summertime is unbelievably dry, so we hiked up the riverbed, using it as our trail and knowing there would not be a single drop of water visible at that time of the year. We hiked over rocks and boulders for hours until we finally reached the top.

At the peak, Sat Nam Singh found a beautiful, lush, green meadow by the side of the dry riverbed. He brought the four of us together, we held hands in a circle, and he guided us through a group mediation to ground us to the earth. At that point, he asked us all to envision what we most wanted in this world right now in this very moment.

As we were standing there in silence holding hands we suddenly heard a loud, roaring rush of water. Sat Nam Singh squeezed my hand, so I opened my eyes and looked at him. He said, "You did that didn't you?" I said, "I don't know." He asked, "What did you just wish for?" I replied, "Well, we've been hiking for hours, it's in the high 80s, and we're all out of water, so I wished for water." We walked back to the river's edge and water was literally gushing to form a flowing river. We stood there looking at each other, asking, "How is this possible?" I went through every left-brain, linear, logical explanation, and then we filled our canteens, finished our meditation, and spent the rest of the afternoon hiking back downhill by the side of this rushing stream. When we reached the parking lot, the stream went into the ground and disappeared.

Daniel and Sat Nam Singh moved to different areas and we lost touch, but Patricia and I still talk about that day as if it were yesterday. It was a pivotal moment in all of our lives. I still can't explain the way the water showed up. I had no expectation, and did not think much about what I wanted. It was one of those moments you read about in books but that you don't think is real, yet all four of us experienced it.

The magnitude of this experience changed my life. I realized we can manifest anything. All we have to do is think it and wish it, and then it could be ours. Instead, we tend to feel our heads with doubt, fears, and everything except for the Light. That day I discovered something amazing simply by following the instructions of a maintenance man.

Before this incident, my life was based purely on business. I had my own company—a real estate management firm—and the single most important thing to me was the bottom line. I was already a seeker but one filled with doubt and hope. I knew what I wanted life to be, but it was never put to me in such simplistic terms as "Wish it and it can be yours." That manifestation helped me to understand that it really is that easy.

My life changed for the better, as I realized that it's not all about the dollars. That simple experience gave me a sense of connectedness. I knew I was not separate from God, and that I was part of something magnificent. I was 29 years old at the time and it was such a gift to be able to take that knowledge and wisdom into my life and say, "Okay, now what?!" During the times when I get sucked back into the system, into business, into the chase for success and money, I now catch myself and return to that memorable moment in the meadow.

That day as we hiked on our path up the mountain, we saw no other hikers, yet we knew there must be many more people joining us on the climb. With a mountain that big and a life this big, there must be many paths up the mountain. Yet from our perspective, at the bottom of the mountain, it can sometimes appear that we're the only one climbing up. I've learned that it's not until we get high enough up the mountain on our own path that we see there are multiple paths all leading to the same place.

The experience led me to the realization that there are many paths to God, or the Divine energy, leading to the same place. It has taught me acceptance and tolerance and changed my philosophy from religious to spiritual. It has been a guiding truth that no matter what happens in life, I can always close my eyes and relive that experience. That day has helped me grow into the person I now am. I am deeply grateful for the experience.

SHIRAH S. PENN
Spiritual Teacher, Workshop Facilitator, and Author
Florida, United States

When I was a little girl I used to attend Friday night services at my Father's shul. He was a Rabbi and I was his first daughter. My mother and I would sit together as my father gave his Friday night sermon. During those times, I felt so close to my father and to God! I experienced the service, the music, the prayers, and the sermon.

As our family grew, I became the big sister to two brothers and we all attended services together. We would not always behave ourselves, however, and that took away the spiritual feeling.

Then, as I became a teenager, I started questioning some of the practices and teachings of my father. I also questioned some of the parenting techniques of my mother. I didn't realize it then, but I needed the love and approval of my parents and they didn't always love me unconditionally.

So I learned that I wasn't good enough and I didn't act in a way my parents approved of sometimes. As a result, my self-esteem suffered.

I enjoyed being a student and decided early on that I wanted to be a teacher. Upon graduating from college, I did become a teacher and married a "nice Jewish man." However, I still didn't feel good about myself.

In 1971, I received a Masters degree from the University of Miami, along with a divorce from my husband. At this time I decided to go inside myself to find out what was wrong with me. I went to many seminars and lectures. I read countless books, and attended workshops.

In 1981, I met a group of women who had a special glow about them, as if they were surrounded by light. I wanted to be like them so I asked them, "How did you get to be so confident?" They told me about a seminar called Insight Transformational Seminars, and there was one coming up in Miami.

I decided to attend this seminar, and as a result of the loving and caring I experienced there I learned to take responsibility for my thoughts and feelings. I learned that the Universe rewards action, not thought, and I discovered that I *am* good enough. I realized that I was worthy and capable of giving and receiving love, just like everyone else. The additional Insight Trainings helped me to transform many family relationships.

I experienced being in the Light, and my connection to the Higher Power, the Source energy, God. It dawned on me that I had always had this connection and now I wanted to share my love.

That is why after retiring from 42 years in teaching, I still have an urge to connect Lightworkers and teach others how to get in touch with their energy and loving presence. What I learned most of all is that we don't acknowledge ourselves enough. So now it is my turn to share what I have learned with others. Love yourself and love each other...

RICHARD HARVEY

Psycho-Spiritual Psychotherapist and Spiritual Teacher
Orgiva, Spain

All Was Light: All Was Consciousness

For most people, spiritual awakening is a process, but for some it can happen in an instant. Illogical and nonsensical as this contradiction appears, it *is* true. When you happen upon paradox and contradiction there are two possibilities: either you have fallen into Lewis Carroll land—the world of the Jabberwocky and Alice—or you have entered the world of the sacred; the spiritual domain where time meets eternity. You occupy two places simultaneously, there at the border. You reach the end of duality and the beginning of the sphere of Unity, and just before you tip over into it completely, you teeter on the edge of two worlds.

Wonderful accounts of adepts who awakened in a single instant may be found in all spiritual traditions. The sound of stones striking bamboo, the color of plum blossoms, the sight of a falling leaf, or a single spoken word can be enough to illuminate the mind and heart forever. Shakyamuni Buddha, for example, was enlightened at the sight of the morning star.

When I was a young aspiring spiritual student I sought the experience of instantaneous Samadhi. Immediate enlightenment sounded too good to be true. But slowly I came to realize that my awakenings could more correctly be called *reminders* or *remembering*, for my spiritual journey was less a search and more a patient waiting for it to find me. From as far back as I can remember I was a companion to Divinity. I recall it in the shapes and the shiny-ness of matter in my early childhood, in the magic of nature in my adolescence, and in the sparkling atmospheres and movement of the invisible through my 20s. Today, I am a spiritual teacher. I teach what I have always known.

A Vessel Surrendered to the Divine

This account of spiritual awakening is not the only mystical experience I have had, and in some ways it may not be the most powerful or awe-inspiring. I have sometimes reflected on how my most powerful awakenings have often been the most mundane—experiences that are extremely hard to communicate, because there's usually such an inward intensity and heightened elation that defies outward expression, and is devoid of drama.

This awakening story may not be the most life-changing, but it was the most life-challenging. Not only is it as fabulous as a movie in content, variety, and spectacle (probably a French movie from the '60s, slow moving with the sounds of a tranquil countryside setting), but it also defied many of my personal views and prejudices, for I have a strong sub-personality whom I call Doubting Thomas. Though an apostle, he really doesn't believe until he has placed his hand in the wound! The domain of fairies, nature divas, elemental images perceived anthropomorphically, vulnerability taken to the nth degree—none of this was my natural milieu. Grounded spirituality was more my stance. I preferred the earth beneath my feet before I felt my head in the clouds. So this experience shook my prejudices to the core. It was like being held in the hand of God and having all my reasoning, my rigidity, and my fears shaken out of me until all that was left was a vessel of transformation surrendered to the Divine.

Seized with the Fear of Death

One day, I was walking in a forest with my teacher and two companions. I was observing nature closely, greatly absorbed. The air was soaked in a rare atmosphere. I can only describe it as wisdom or illumination; a pregnancy, a portentousness, and a promise of wisdom and revelation.

Coming around a bend into a beautiful glade, I became entranced by the sunlight dancing and twinkling over a dazzling, flowing stream of clear water. As I lowered myself toward the gentle flow, I could see the pebbles shining magically beneath the gurgling water. They were luminous, their various shapes and colors mesmerizing. Brilliant bubbles filled with sunlight exploded all over the surface of the water. It was all so beautiful and transcendent, full of enchantment, and as I sought to get even closer I inadvertently dipped my face into the water. I took a breath and unexpectedly sucked in water instead of air.

I can't tell you why or how or really what happened then, because I fell into an alternative reality. The air, the atmosphere, the teacher, the wisdom hovering in the air, everything combined and was somehow conspiring to teach a deeper sacred level of Truth. I was seized with a tremendous fear of death. I was utterly terrified. I panicked, absolutely petrified. I shook and trembled and as I felt myself being pulled up off the ground; my knees shook so much I could hardly stand.

Miracles Took Place All Around Me

I leapt back from the stream, crying like a newborn baby. I was totally open. My teacher laughed insanely and paddled water up into my face with his hands as I wept. When the crying stopped, I stood still for a long time.

The air around me was profoundly still and filled with Being, with God. Miracles took place all around me. Off to my right, a bonfire appeared on the water, just beyond my physical vision (later, I read in the I Ching that fire over water represents renewal and transformation, the edge of change, spring, and re-birth). A band of incredible beings—elves, fairies, dwarves, oversized mice, and assorted animals—clothed in their finery, filed into the glade behind me carrying leafy boughs and armfuls of flowers. They began to play drums, cymbals, flutes, and shaking bells. Somehow

I "saw" this without turning around. What can I say about such a sight and such music? It was like nothing I had ever seen or heard! Of another time, another world and dimension, of another level of existence entirely, the atmosphere they conveyed and inhabited was magical, enchanted, mercurial. As I listened, my senses seemed to merge into a shimmering light. When they had finished playing, we wandered off. Somehow I was leading now. My teacher and two companions alongside, behind, or around me felt spiritually supportive, and somehow deeply necessary, numinous even, to everything that happened that day.

We passed by a field, and the scene of a medieval battle was played out before me, from the first thunderous charge to the silent stillness of the slain. It was so extraordinary, but I didn't for a minute consider the momentousness of what I witnessed. It simply *was*, like an imprint or an impression of energies from another time, yet ethereally real and present.

Accidentally, I stepped in a cowpat and created the most beautiful pattern of shape, texture, and color, in which I saw God. God in a cowpat seemed like a cosmic joke. We all laughed ecstatically. I saw the Divine everywhere. I walked in the sunlight through the fields, over the gates, and among the trees, and everywhere everything was sacred, beautiful, blissful, and blessed. Gratitude welled up in my heart and surged through me. I became heart. I became love. I became devotion, and through my tears I was filled with passion and love for the whole of life.

In the Field of Eternity

The walk through the glade and the field, along the paths and lanes, was utter delight—gentle, sensitive, holy, and timeless. My consciousness was filled with total acceptance and compassion. I had entered a Divine state of ecstasy, bliss, and worship. When we emerged onto a tarmac lane nothing changed. Essentially, I experienced no differentiation whatsoever. We strolled along a lane that led to a pub set in the countryside. As we strolled in through the gate, a driver was steering his car out of the car park. I remember looking straight through him. I could read his mind. His expectation was that we should move out of his way, but we kept on walking straight toward the car, merely noticing it, witnessing it as a phenomenon, a neutral event. Though this was years ago, I can close my eyes today and experience the events as I did on that day. The objective phenomenon of the car and driver was no different from the pebbles, the sunshine, and the gratitude that filled me: it was exactly the same as gazing at a star, a flower, or a flowing stream! Merely neutral, unbiased, arising form. The driver's face changed as he saw me and slowed his car and his anger, which was the conditioned reaction, his automatic behavior toward people who strolled in front of his moving car. He had entered my energy field, the field of eternity, and in that moment I walked past his car and into the grounds of the pub.

I became aware that tears were streaming down my cheeks. They had been since I had inhaled the water at the stream. The world was deeply affecting, heartbreaking, and heart-opening. It was so strong and magnificent, fragile and vulnerable, somehow all at the same time. I could feel the whole world and it was so full of hope and drama, action and eventfulness, playfulness and pathos, light, consciousness, and peace.

We approached a typical English beer garden with wooden tables and seats, garden umbrellas for shade, and lots of people: singles, couples, friends, families, and larger groups, chatting, laughing, smiling, in serious conversation, creating a buzz of gentle excitement, drinking, eating, and conversing together on a midsummer's evening. Looking back, I have no idea why no one even looked up at me, how I didn't disturb or draw the attention of a single person there. The four of us simply drifted toward a vacant table and sat down, as if we were invisible.

Fascination with the Ordinary World

When our drinks were brought I realized I was in an extreme form of a state I had experienced before. It was a state I can best describe as fascination with the ordinary world of everyday objects. I had first experienced this following a meditation retreat. Returning to London after several days of intensive meditation I had walked into the bay window area of my room and been profoundly struck by the phenomenon of my antique wooden desk. It was such a familiar object to me and yet in that moment I experienced it as if I had never seen it before, as if I had no idea what purpose it served, or what its function was. I slumped in the chair and examined the pens, pencils, desk lamp, and assorted objects before me similarly, with innocence and fascination. On this occasion I had reached an edge of tolerance. The gentle, open position of the observer entirely liberated from any preconception, thought, or previous understanding, memory, or past met an earthy, sensible, practical aspect of me. And I pulled myself back from the brink of intense presence or idiocy (depending on which part of me was looking at it) and opted for a return to functioning as a human being in the world. As soon as I did this I felt immensely sad, as if I was leaving my true home and making a great sacrifice; as if I was forsaking all that was familiar and truly consonant with my being by accepting the human condition.

The Light of Transformation

At the pub table covered with drinks, it was a different story. I was way beyond the place where I had turned back, sitting at my desk in London. The glasses, the liquids they contained, the little bowl in the center of the table, the pole supporting the umbrella, were all Divine manifestations of love. I was entranced by everything: an insect floating over the table, an eruption of laughter from a nearby table, the fragrance of the flowers. Then of course there was the light. Both the sunlight low on the horizon now casting sublime, mysterious shadows all around our sacred gathering and casting subtle hues of pink and red and green between the tables and connecting us all, and the other light...the light which suffused everything, which did not emanate from the physical sun but shot through everything. This light was the light of transformation, the light of unity, the light of compassion and love and devotion, and in this light everything rested and was fed and nourished and suffused with Divinity. I breathed in a deep draft of air and *knew*. Eternity was now.

The Boundless State of Endless Gratitude

What binds all the events of the spiritual awakening I have recounted here together is the boundless state of endless gratitude I felt. This gratitude deepened and expanded into eternal devotion, not just to someone, something, or selected events, but to All. The clearest thing about this spiritual initiation was that I experienced *no differentiation whatsoever*. Life, death, me, the other, good, bad—it had all faded and gone. It was not there at all. I was free of all dilemma. All was light; all was consciousness. A moment can be all it takes to release us: I took a breath and sucked in water. The rest was a penetrating, luminous beam of radiant love.

MOLLY ANN FAIRLEY
Psychic
London, United Kingdom

When I was 43, a wife and mother, I went through an unexpected and illuminating "psychic opening." I was visited by a young lady called Jane who told me she had received a message from Spirit. Jane exclaimed that I should prepare myself for an exceptional event that would take place in two days and that it was my destiny for it had been written in the Akashic Records. I later found out that the Akashic Records are the spiritual records that hold all of the information about each and every one of us in the higher realms of the super-conscious world. It seems that I had agreed to the "psychic opening" many lifetimes ago. Spirit had, however, moved the date forward, deeming me ready.

It was to begin at 8 p.m. on Thursday evening and continue right through the night. Jane had been chosen as the earth helper who would support me. I didn't know Jane, and I had never seen her before that day. She had been sent by a friend. Surprised and nervous, I overwhelmed Jane with questions. *What was going to happen? How would it happen? Would it hurt? How long would it take? Why me? What had I done to deserve this?* I felt naturally apprehensive. *Did this make me special? Or was that just an ego trip?*

I had always been drawn to psychics and mediums. I wondered how they could possibly know the things they did. Captivated, I attended different psychic circles and began to bring developing psychics home with me. Small groups of spiritually minded people gathered to witness a medium enter into a deep trance, become someone else, and channel spiritual messages. One evening psychic surgery was performed right in front of us. It was riveting stuff.

A Chinese Guide

I first encountered Chinese Woman a short while after the first spiritual meetings at my house. Chinese Woman was a Chinese Guide channeled by Stephanie, a new member to the group. Stephanie was unforgettable. She had passion and a powerful shamanic energy. She had piercing blue eyes and long, shiny brown hair. Men were captivated by her, and I was mesmerized by her incredible ability to transform into a spiritual being. She would speak with a foreign accent that no one could possibly have made up.

Some weeks later, the phone began to ring with people I did not know telling me they had felt drawn to call me. They kept asking me if an important spiritual meeting would be taking place soon. I didn't understand, and yet, it was as if some unseen force from above was directing these people to ring me. Confused, and still wondering how they were finding me, I eventually said yes. I invited Stephanie to come along and speak to a select few. I naturally felt apprehensive and questioned my sanity. What had I let myself in for? They, on the other hand, did not seem at all perturbed. At last, the day of the meeting arrived. Everyone turned up on time, which was unusual in itself. They all told me they had felt drawn to come and they didn't know why. We waited silently with baited breath for what seemed like ages until Stephanie (a.k.a. Chinese Woman) was ready.

At precisely 11 minutes past 11 a.m. on July 11, 1991 (which all adds up to the number 11: the master spiritual number), we heard a faint shuffling and movement upstairs. Stephanie, in the guise of Chinese Woman, descended the stairs one by one as if her feet were tiny and bound. We all wanted to giggle and there were some really odd looks flying across the room as Chinese Woman entered. Stephanie, with her eyes closed, shuffled her way to a chair that had been especially placed there for her.

Stephanie's whole body had taken on the air of a very old woman. Her accent was Chinese and her speech was ancient, as if it came from another time. Chinese Woman addressed the group and welcomed everyone as she began to tell them why they were all there. Afterwards, she opened the meeting to questions. For nearly an hour we asked question after question, some about ourselves and our own soul path, some about our families and our friends' personal lives, and many about the world. We were spellbound. Finally, Chinese Woman departed; shuffling back slowly, hunched over, she ascended the stairs.

A Life-Changing Experience

That day changed my entire life. It was impossible to ignore what I had seen. It would not go away and neither would Stephanie. She remembered little of what had taken place during her trance and it took a while for her to become fully conscious again. I let her rest. Little did I know that she and Chinese Woman were about to play a very important role in my life, and there would be no going back!

Two weeks later Jane turned up for my "psychic opening." She brought an assortment of oils and candles with her and asked where I could spend the night comfortably. She told me that I was to be opened as a psychic channel and trance medium and that I would be able to perform psychic surgery and heal others. She also said that I would become clairvoyant and be able to bring important news to others. Later, I was to become a metaphysical teacher and writer and travel extensively. She said I would be a teacher of psychic healing, psychic studies, and mediumship. I had not been born psychic, so I would be able relate to those who wanted to develop.

It all seemed a bit far-fetched. I was frightened and in a complete daze. I had just gone through a divorce and was only just recovering from the intense fear and identity crisis of going from a typical middle-class Surrey housewife to a single woman earning her own living. I also had a 14-year-old daughter who wouldn't be comfortable with all this odd spiritual stuff.

My Past Lives

Jane asked me to lie down and told me that the "opening process" was about to begin. I lay down nervously. Almost immediately, I began to see images whirling around my mind of my life, childhood, and lives I had never seen before, at first vague but then brightly colored. I shivered with cold in front of an open fire, wrapped in a thick blanket. One moment I was freezing cold and shivering, the next I was hot and sweaty. Jane brought me water and more blankets as my temperature soared up and down.

Throughout the night, I saw lifetime after lifetime, more than 80 in total. I saw each of my deaths and the decisions I had made at the end of each lifetime. I saw all of the events that had led to those decisions and I saw all the people I had met—some of whom I have met in this lifetime. I saw skins being shed from my body, and there were also changes to my hearing. At times it felt like someone was operating on me with a team in the background. I could hear them talking to each other in spirit, issuing each other instructions. I was drifting in and out of consciousness. Bits of me were being connected to other bits, and new bits were being put in.

At times, I found myself in physical or emotional pain. Physical injuries from the past were remembered, rapidly dissolving as they left my body. Emotions such as fear, sadness, anger, and futility came up and passed through me in waves. Emotion after emotion built up inside me before breaking out in great sighs or gut-wrenching tears. It was a similar experience to giving birth. By 6 a.m. I was exhausted and confused. Jane told me it was over, and then she left. I slept until 9 a.m., when my boyfriend came over to see me. I was tearful and in shock and I told him about the images I had seen. By this time images of Christ had started flooding through. It was my 45th birthday and I no longer knew who I was, and neither did he. It was a very difficult time for us both and sadly we decided to separate for some time to adjust.

The next two months were a difficult period of my life. I was unable to cope with much sound so I needed to stay near to the house. One day, after six weeks had passed, I remember going to Brighton on the south coast of England and not being able to stay near the beach. I was driven right to the top where the pavement overlooks a small fairground on the front. The noise was deafening and I had to come home. Light overwhelmed my eyes and I became sensitive to the slightest change. I kept the curtains closed for weeks. Physically, I felt more tired than I had ever been, even in late pregnancy. On the odd trip out, I would need to sit on walls after short walks, rather like an old lady.

Psychic Energy Flashes

Daily, I saw energies out of the corners of my eyes, which resembled tiny sparks. My emotions were sensitive and raw. I could feel people's energy, moods, and thoughts through my stomach, which was totally new to me. I instantly knew if someone was being dishonest. My intuition had been cranked up hundreds of times and I seemed to "know" so many things that I had not known before. It felt as if I had one mind in my head and another in my stomach. I could feel where my aura started and stopped, where it was picking up information, and how it was constantly moving. Sometimes I saw colors too, but I had no idea what they meant.

In the midst of all this, Stephanie moved in. She arrived one day about a week after "that night," carrying a small brown leather suitcase and a message from Chinese Woman. She was to stay for two months until I was well. Well? I did not know that I was ill. Stephanie told me she had channeled a huge spiritual frequency conversion and that it had shaken me to the core of my being.

Unknowingly I Had Been Prepared

Apparently, my body had been prepared for this spiritual conversion for years, but it had still been an enormous shock to my body and mind. I was told it would take time to heal. Then I remembered how I had thought it strange that I suddenly studied yoga at the age of 30 and rapidly became a teacher after having only ever worked in an office before that.

What I found even stranger was that this happened because of a series of nervous breakdowns that had called an abrupt halt to my then overzealous need to work all the hours God provides. No doctor or specialist could fathom the cause of these breakdowns. On the allotted day, however, I remember finding a book called *Peace from Nervous Suffering* by Dr. Claire Weekes, and on page 87 I found the answer to my nervous breakdowns. I read it, I understood it, and then I was cured.

Now, all these years later, it all fit together like a jigsaw puzzle. Without the grueling workouts and mental ordeals I had endured whilst training to be a yoga teacher, I would not have been fit enough to have sustained the frequency changes or mentally strong enough for the emotions to flow.

It was a relief to have Stephanie living with me. She was light-hearted and fun to be around. She took over the cooking and the housework, leaving me able to ask as many questions as I wished. She told me that food would be provided, as I could not leave the house. Food was delivered to the door each day, which she said came from Spirit. I never did find out who the real earth benefactor was.

She told me light-hearted stories about Spirit and the playful things the baby Earth Spirits like to do. Under the constant guidance of Stephanie and, on occasion, Chinese Woman, I felt thoroughly supported and spoiled. Stephanie spoke in riddles or stories when she wanted me to learn something, which kept me guessing. I was often made to wait for the answer until I knew it myself intuitively. This strengthened me and heightened my ability to work psychically and intuitively. Miraculously, within five weeks of Stephanie's arrival, I was conducting psychic surgery as a trance medium and bringing through messages in front of small groups.

MICHAEL ROADS
Author
Queensland, Australia

When I was 29 years old, I ruptured a disc in my lower spine. For two decades, the pain in my lower back caused me prolonged and agonizing suffering. If I had three consecutive pain-free months, I considered myself fortunate. My daily life was haunted by both chronic and acute back pain.

At the age of 40, I was involved in a metaphysical experience with an advanced Being who was mentoring me. I asked if we could come to an agreement. The Being looked at me inquiringly, and I said, "I want to either be enlightened by the age of 50, or else dead." I was fully committed. I did not want to play the pain game any longer than 50. I was fully prepared to die, and come back again. If I gave it my all, I figured that I could awaken within those 10 years. The Being studied me intently for long moments, and then nodded.

Nine dramatic years of pain and suffering passed. By now I had now developed a very distressing condition called cellulitis, caused by stress. In my case I had it in my face. Cellulitis is the swelling of the subcutaneous tissue of the affected area. It would always follow the same path into my left ear, both of my eyes, my nostrils, my left cheek, my lips, and finally, into my mouth. All of these areas would swell, and turn a bright red color. It was not painful, but because all the swollen areas included under-the-skin itching, it was very distressing. It had reached the stage where it would quickly get into my nostrils, causing them to swell so I could not breathe through my nose. When it got into my mouth, I could feel my tongue swelling. Then it would reach into my throat. When my throat began to swell, breathing became very difficult, and suffocation was a real threat.

One sunny morning in July 1986, I opened my eyes, only to squeeze them shut again in anguish. I was having another attack of cellulitis. Plus, I could hardly move with lower back pain. Then, amazingly, from within the dark depths of despair, came a light of brilliant intensity flooding me. It was as though I saw myself clearly. This was it—crunch time. I was 49 and three months. Reaching 50 seemed to no longer be an option. For most of my life I had taken my body to doctors or naturopaths to heal, and ultimately they could not heal me. I *knew* that it was time for me to take full responsibility for my body, and my health. In this moment of Truth and Insight, I *knew* that I could heal myself. The problem was, I had no idea *how* to do it!

I told Treenie, my late wife. I asked her to promise me that she would not bring in any doctors or healers. No matter how bad the cellulitis got, either I healed myself, or I would suffocate and die. Treenie knew about my agreement, and was not at all happy with it. Nevertheless, she nodded. "If that is how you want it, I have little choice but to agree." With that, she kissed me, and walked back to the kitchen.

Instead of feeling elated, I felt shocked. Suddenly, a memory ignited of an incident eight years earlier. I had been in deep meditation for several hours, when the relationship between God and myself was suddenly and abruptly erased. All of my inner feelings about God were somehow annihilated. I felt as though God had abandoned me. My intellect assured me that God would not abandon me, but emotionally, that is exactly what it felt like. I felt so shocked that I literally fell out of the meditation. For the next two days I could not relate to anyone, so profound was my inner sense of loss. Through the years that followed I missed my childish God musings, along with my more mature adult thoughts and feelings—they had all gone. Only emptiness remained.

Eight years ago I had felt abandoned by God, and now I felt abandoned by Treenie. I knew she loved me, but she was abandoning me. This shocking sense of abandonment stayed with me, making me feel miserable. It was completely unexpected. Food for the cellulitis! My inner feeling that I could heal myself remained, but it was squashed and reduced by unrealized abandonment issues.

No dramatic healing took place. Instead, over the next two days my lower back pain intensified, and the cellulitis continued to worsen. Despite this, the inner knowing that I could heal myself persisted. The problem was, I did not have a "How to Heal Myself" manual! Most of the time I was confined to bed, but on the third day, making a heroic effort, I managed to drag myself out of bed and crawl onto the verandah. I was sprawled in extreme discomfort on an old sofa when my friend Yvonne called in for a chat.

"My God! You look rough, Michael," she said.

I told her that despite appearances, I was healing myself. Yvonne raised her eyebrows, but said nothing. At that very moment, Treenie appeared in the front doorway.

"Michael believes that he grows through pain and suffering. This is the result!" I had heard her say these exact words hundreds of times throughout the last 10 or so years, and I always dismissed them. Now, for the very first time, the words entered my heart and soul. They truly penetrated into my very Being: "I believe that I grow through pain and suffering!"

Oh, my God! If, over all these years I have held a subconscious belief that this is how I grow, then with the strength and passion of my commitment to inner growth, I am the creator of all my pain and suffering over all these years. I was in shock. I thought back to the words of Jean, a visiting spiritual mentor from earlier years. "Michael," she said, "you have lost your joy." Wrong. I had never had any joy! I had been happy, but real joy? A joy that spoke of living by grace? I had never experienced that. Neither had I ever experienced peace. The peace that removes one from all anxiety, all worry. If I believed that I grew through pain and suffering, how could I experience joy, or love, or peace? Such a belief was the very denial of love and joy and peace. I was stunned. But I recognized and knew it as an undeniable Truth.

I stared at Yvonne, my thoughts whirling. Only about eight weeks ago she had asked me what love is, revealing to me that I did not know. It occurred to me that, in the way of life, I had been set up. She had asked me a question that I had never honestly asked myself. Because of her question, I *knew* that I did not know what love is. I had asked myself, "Who am I?" But I had never asked, "What is love?" Now, it was far too late.

It was my moment of Truth. A lifetime of false beliefs stood exposed.

For long moments, I faltered, lost in my self-deceit. *What do I do now?* As soon as I posed that question, I was gripped by a fierce desire to face myself. I wanted to look into a mirror and see *me*; my self-deceit, my failure, my pain, my suffering. I wanted to see the revealed, exposed *raw me*. I wanted to say to this unconcealed me, "I love you."

I painfully crawled in a crabwise shuffle from the verandah and into the bedroom of my youngest son, where he had a large mirror on the floor, propped against the wall. With my eyes closed, I slumped to the floor in front of the mirror. I wanted to get the full impact of saying "I love you."

I opened my eyes. The face that stared back at me had four days' growth of beard, and was grotesquely swollen with cellulitis. Heavy bags of swollen tissue hung under eyes filled with pain and suffering. My left ear resembled a raw steak slapped carelessly onto the side of my head. My jaw hung in a swollen fold, and bright red inflammation quilted my face in all the places of the swelling. My lips were swollen, while inside my mouth I could feel the swelling of my tongue and mouth tissue. My face spoke of loss, despair, suffering, and utter defeat. In this moment of Truth, I knew that it was my creation, the manifestation of all my beliefs. This travesty was the result of my commitment to spiritual growth.

Speechless, I stared at myself in shock. I could not speak or even think the words of love. Tears trickled down my cheeks. I had reached rock bottom. I had made the agreement, so I was ready for my life to end. For all those years of suffering, I had been searching for self-realization, for enlightenment, and that search had reduced me to this—an abject failure.

Deep inside, I surrendered. I did not give up; I gave in. I became aware now of a shadowy door close to the mirror. I knew it was not a physical door, for it was clearly a metaphysical doorway. I knew that through that door was death. I only had to walk my metaphysical self through that metaphysical door and, as agreed, my life would be over.

I was terrified. I had failed, but I had an agreement to honor. My journey was finished. I felt like a husk; there was nothing left. Metaphysically, I attempted to go through the door, but I could not. I knew that first I had to let go of all my attachments. My teenaged children came to mind. I knew that they could all manage without me, even if I was missed. I found this very difficult to do, letting go of them one by one. But I managed it. With many tears and much inner anguish, I managed to let go of them.

I tried again to enter the door. I could not.

I knew then that I had to let go of Treenie. I thought of how easily she had let go of me when I asked her to let me die. Oh my gosh, she had an ability that I was struggling to find. Could I let go of her? Was my emotional attachment too strong? There is no way of describing the long inner struggle I went through, but eventually I let go of Treenie. It was heartbreakingly painful.

Again, I attempted to walk through the shadow door. I could not.

What else was there to let go of? I instantly knew: my desire for enlightenment. That would be easy. All that my desire had produced was an abundance of pain and suffering. Okay, so it did not have to be like that—but that was the way of it! I let go of my desire for enlightenment without any struggle.

Once more, I tried to enter the door. I could not.

Oh, God! What now? Again, an instant knowing—God! *I'm supposed to let go of God? How do I do that?* I remembered my meditation eight years earlier when God let go of me! Was I now really supposed to let go of God? Very clearly, I knew that even if I did think that God had surrendered me, I had not let go of my God attachment. I knew, instantly and uncomfortably, that my fear was clinging to God. Fresh tears slid down my cheeks. *Let go of God! If I let go of God, I won't exist.* I made an inner move toward the door, but the block was unyielding. I had to let go of God. I struggled with this for what felt like a long time, but somehow, in some inexplicable way, I managed the most difficult "letting go" of the whole process. I let go of my God attachment.

Okay, now I can get through that door of death, I thought. I could not.

Now what? There was nothing left! And then, with a sinking sensation, again I knew. I had to surrender me. I remembered the dreams I had been having for the past five nights. They had bothered me. In each dream, I had died. In each dream, after I had died, I was placed in a clear, fast-flowing river. It was my burial place. There was no great drama in the dreams, except that in each dream, I was irrevocably dead. Through the clear rippling water, my body was visible resting on the stones of the riverbed; that was disturbing. One dream of death, okay; two dreams, still okay; but five nights in a row, and in every one of them I am dead, and placed in a clear, fast-flowing river, not okay!

So now what do I do? How, in God's name, do I let go of me? I had no idea. Part of me liked the concept, but I had no clue about how to do it. I did not like me; perhaps that was a start. And to think that all this began when I tried to tell myself that I loved me. In vain I struggled with letting go of me, but nothing happened. I imagined me throwing myself, dead, into the river of my dreams, but nothing happened. I tried and I tried and I tried, until finally, tired and hurting, I gave up on the whole idea. Another failure. Then abruptly, from out of the blue, I knew how. I simply let go. I knew that the me I was struggling to let go of did not exist. The identity-me is an illusion. There is no personal me. And because that me did not exist, letting go was no more than the profound recognition of this Truth.

Certain now, I metaphysically walked to the door—and passed through it.

There was no death. Instead, I walked into a Benediction of Love. I became one with the Benediction of Love and Light. It felt as though I had exploded into Light. I *knew* my Truth. For a time-less no-time, I walked my own timeline, changing certain actions in certain moments in the timelessness of my life path. What a paradox. I have had several incidents in this life when I had been very close to death. Somehow, each suddenly and dramatically changed in the last vital moment—and I lived. I had always as-sumed that it was my guardian angel, busily working overtime in an attempt to keep me alive. Instead, I found that it was my fu-ture awakened Self, walking my own timeline and making all the changes that needed changing to eventually become the person who could make the changes!

I experienced the timeless realization of Self. Spiritual en-lightenment exists only in the eternal moment, never in linear time.

When I returned to a physical and linear reality, I noted that 20 minutes had passed since I had stepped through the now-nonexistent door. I also knew that my identity had indeed died. The ending of a personal illusion, and the awakening to a greater reality.

The cellulitis had gone, never to return. My terrible chronic back pain had gone, never to return. My spine had completely healed, the disc regenerated. My Awakening to Self was the end of anxiety, worry, and stress. Today, I no longer remember what anxiety and worry feel like. I have no fears, no anger, no negative emotional dramas. I have inner peace, inner clarity, inner certainty. Sometimes I feel a little concern about something, but concern is positive; worry is negative—very different. Joy is now an almost constant bubble within. I have also learned that spiritual enlightenment is not the end of inner growth; it is a powerful new beginning.

Beyond all doubt, I now *know* that I am an immortal Being— this is also *your* Truth.

GABRIELLE SCHWARZWALD
Holistic Therapist and Energy Healer
Kent, United Kingdom

The Light Essence

I was born with the gift of healing and I have had many spiritual experiences, such as the night when a mysterious mark appeared on my body when I was a child. This mark is still visible today, and no one has ever been able to tell me or my family what it is and where it came from. Shortly after the mark showed up, electrical items started breaking down in my presence. This made me feel unwell and the only relief came through playing with plants and animals.

My dad was diagnosed with terminal cancer in 1983 and was given six weeks to live. My family was devastated when the specialist broke this terrible news to us. I saw my angel appear to me, like she did when I was growing up, and with her guidance I placed my hands where they were needed. I loved my dad beyond words and for the first time I consciously used these healing abilities combined with unconditional love. The cancer "burned away" until it had completely gone, giving my dad an extra seven years to live. From that time onwards I opened my mind and began a wonderful journey, studying constantly to search for ways to gain knowledge and understand the wonderful universal energies that are available to help regain the body's own healing abilities.

Along with my guardian angel and my main guide, many other wonderful guides, spirit doctors, and masters joined me on my journey, teaching me the ancient universal knowledge that is implanted in my soul—a knowledge that we all possess deep inside.

The healing and other abilities developed as I learned from my lessons and experiences. At times I was rewarded by witnessing the manifestation of my guardian angel, guides, and masters. Today, many guides and spirit people have chosen transfiguration by using my face and sometimes body to show themselves to my clients if it is appropriate for their healing.

In March 1993, I went into labor with my beautiful son. I had complications, hemorrhaged, collapsed, and my heart stopped beating. During this time, I had a near-death experience (NDE) and I was given a glimpse of what is beyond evolution in a universal sense. While I was on the other side I saw many visions of Mother Earth, history, humanity, environmental changes, and economical changes in the spiral through time and space. Most of what I saw has come to pass in the years that followed.

Shortly after my near-death experience I had a car accident. A drunken young driver hurtled towards me at high speed. There was nowhere to turn to get out of his way. I heard my angel telling me to protect my face, get my knees as close as I could to my body, and relax, which helped immensely when the frontal impact occurred.

A few months later we moved to England. I was still very tired and exhausted from the birth and the accident, and at times had to use a wheelchair when I had no feeling in my legs. My ex-husband came across a book that later had a huge influence on my life. The book was by Betty Shine, an author, medium, and healer with worldwide recognition for her outstanding work. After I finished reading her book, I contacted her straight away for healing. Betty was no longer doing any mediumship nor giving readings but she made an exception with me and had been waiting for me to contact her. The reading was amazing. She picked up on my birth, my angel, the mark on my body, and my NDE. My health improved drastically and we became good friends.

Betty told me to start my spiritual work in England immediately, which I did by joining the original Rainbow Healing Group founded by a wonderful lady named Ms. Joan D. Joan's dream was to build a healing center for people from all walks of life. Later, she found a mansion that would provide this service. People came first from the surrounding towns. The word spread fast and soon people turned up from across the country.

A lady came who was desperate to have a baby. She had tried for many years but was not able to hold a pregnancy for longer than 12 weeks. This lady had endured 15 miscarriages and had to undergo many tests and treatments that conventional medicine had to offer, but nothing had worked. After a medium told her she would have a child she came to see me at the center. I worked with her and one day I felt a little heartbeat as I held my hands over her abdomen. I knew she had conceived but did not want to tell anyone until the fourth month. A magazine editor heard about it and the story went public. The BBC invited us to talk about this so-called miracle baby on the Kilroy Show.

I did not want to go but Betty Shine gave me the confidence to represent the spiritual work and the healing we do. I was scared to go public, but Betty reassured me that everything would be fine. She told me that the words would come easily. After a few months I accepted the offer to go on the show. At that time the lady was eight months pregnant. There were many medical professionals and healers present and my mind was blank, but as soon as the show started my angel took over and the words positively flowed during the discussion.

A few days later the BBC called telling me they had to employ more staff to operate the phones as calls flooded in asking for me. I was surprised when huge bags of healing requests arrived on my doorstep too.

I worked day and night to answer them all. Some were so heartbreaking. I knew I could not help everybody and that some of those wonderful people were dying. All I could do was help them with pain relief and their transition to the other side. People visited the center and my home from everywhere, even from abroad. I worked hard for years, for no fee. The best reward was to be able to help with my gift of healing and see a smile on the face of the terminally ill people whose only hope was to receive a little pain relief. Some of those beautiful souls were healed instantly, whereas others took slightly longer, and the destiny of some souls was clearly to go "home." I received loving feedback from relatives and clients and many referred to the same phenomena during their distant healing sessions. They all described my angel, some described my healing guides, and others described me right down to what I was wearing at the time of the distant healing. At that time, in 1997, I was told that my speech and discussion with the medical profession at the show were the driving forces for healing to be finally acknowledged in hospitals and by the National Health Service in the UK.

I had many beautiful spiritual experiences during my enlightening journey, and each one is very dear to my heart and soul. In 2009, I met Andrew. Andrew had cancer in his neck and he came on an almost daily basis to get his medication at the pharmacy where I worked at the time. His tumor was inoperable. At first Andrew did not believe in healing but when a second tumor grew on the other side of his neck and the doctor told him it was cancerous, he approached me for healing. We started the healing one Monday for five minutes. He could not believe the intense magnetic energy coming from my hands. We did the next session on a Wednesday morning, the day of his scan. Andrew came in on Friday morning with such a big smile on his face, and at that moment I knew he had good news to share. Andrew hugged me and said the scan was clear, the second tumor had completely gone and the first one had shrunk. I gave him another healing session, again for only five minutes. The remaining tumor disappeared in no time, and a year later Andrew was given the all-clear.

I saw Andrew again in 2011; he was still clear and enjoying every moment of life with his partner. I contacted him again weeks after our meeting. He told me he had a strange dream, in which he saw an angel reaching out and holding his hands. The angel's touch was like an electric shock and it reminded him of the healing. The healing experience changed his life forever, making him a firm believer in the mystical realms of the angelic force, and the possibility that our body can heal itself with a little help from above.

Another wonderful experience I would like to share was when a beautiful soul from New York contacted me on a social networking site in summer 2011. Rose asked if I was able to give her an online reading. We had never met or spoken to each other before. I felt a warm glow in my solar plexus and immediately I started to write words that were of great importance to her. I had no idea what I was writing and I sent it to her without even reading it myself. I did not hear anything for a few days, and then an e-mail arrived. Rose told me she was shocked and had to digest what I sent to her as each word described her life right up to this day. Information I had given her started to take shape within a few days of receiving the reading.

As with everything in my spiritual life there is a reason for it all. During the following months Rose's life became terribly hectic, flying backwards and forwards from the United States to England. Her whole life was a rollercoaster. I stayed in contact with her to help her get through it all until we finally met.

I also knew she was ill and in constant pain. However, after we met in Brighton I was pretty shocked when Rose told me she suffered from a dreadful autoimmune disease called scleroderma. This illness caused intense pain in her hands, feet, and her whole body. Her hands were icy cold and the conditions were creeping up her arms. I gave her the first healing session. The blue color disappeared instantly and her hands warmed up. I had never seen this condition before. Rose was diagnosed in 1999 and she was on 42 different medications daily to keep her alive. She had to return to New York and we saw each other again towards the end of the year. I treated Rose with reflexology and healing. Since then her body stayed warm, and Rose finally came off the medication. She said the healing accomplished in just three sessions what no doctor was able to do for her in 13 years. Rose finally married the English man she loves, and she is now living a healthy life with her husband in the UK.

Through Rose I met Tracy, a remarkable woman who healed herself from breast and ovarian cancer many years ago without any conventional treatment. Tracy came to see me for a chakra alignment and energy healing. During the chakra balancing I felt my face changing, which is not unusual for me. My body became physically lighter. I heard the singing voice of my angel and felt her intense presence. I thought I was going to fly. Tracy saw it happening and watched me closely. When I give healing I know I am guided, taken over by my angel and healing guides, but this time it was different. This time it was for both of us to see.

My face and body became more transparent during the healing; I was unable to influence what was about to happen, nor able to control the speed of my hands. I stepped completely out of my body, this time fully aware of what was going on when my body became lighter and more transparent, until we both saw my hands and arms disappearing. Tracy witnessed my angel manifest with a wonderful warm glow of golden and vibrant green colors.

This did not happen in a meditative trance or dream state, but on a completely consciousness level. It was such a fantastic, magical moment. So much love and light was present that it filled the whole room for days after!

Chapter 3:
Messages from Spirit/Synchronicity

I love receiving messages from Spirit, as they give me a peaceful feeling of being on-course in my life, and they bring a sense of feeling loved, cared for, and protected. When I was putting together *The Light: A Book of Wisdom*, I was shown so many signs that I would wake up in the morning wondering what messages I would be gifted with in the day ahead. Life became very exciting and full of the most delightful surprises.

One day I decided to break up my computer work with a stroll on the beach, which was just across the road from the apartment where I lived at the time in Spain. I stepped into some flip flops, rubbed a little sun cream onto my face, and then set off. At the beach I immediately took off my flip flops and stepped onto the sand, relishing the feeling of the little grains oozing between my toes. I headed down to the ocean and began to walk in the cooling tide, in the direction of the lighthouse, a good 45 minutes away. As I walked, *The Light* was very much on my mind, and doubts began to show up, as I wondered if I was doing the right thing in putting together the book. I worried that I may be wasting my time and that it may never sell any copies, or that people might not understand it, or like it. I tried letting the fears go by throwing them into the sea, but more kept cropping up.

Two key messages or signs came my way that day. The first was that, as my thoughts rattled on, I happened to see a white feather in the sand. I bent down to pick it up and my initial thought was that it may be from an angel trying to tell me that everything would be okay, and to ignore any doubts I had about *The Light*. However, then I noticed a flock of seagulls flying overhead and decided that's where the white feather must have come from. When I returned home, it was so hot that I opened my balcony door a fraction to let some air in. I went into the kitchen to get a glass of water and when I returned there was a little white feather right in the middle of the living room floor. I picked it up to inspect it and immediately observed that it was such a beautiful and pure shade of white that it practically glowed. My heart stirred and I realized that I was being taught a massive lesson in self-doubt. My first feeling about the feather on the beach—being a sign from the angels—was totally correct. I had no reason to doubt that. And in the same way, I had no reason to doubt my guidance to bring out *The Light*.

The second message I received that day was related to the same lesson. A little further along my walk, after the feather discovery, a white moth appeared out of nowhere and started flying directly in front of me, along the tide. Every once in a while it would stop on a pebble, and then when I'd caught it up it would fly off again, leading me further along the tide, closer and closer to the lighthouse. This went on for some time, until I realized that it was a sure sign from Spirit and that the launch of *The Light* was a pivotal part of my own spiritual journey.

There have been so many signs and synchronicities in the last few years that it is impossible to mention them all here, but another big one took place when I was deciding the title of *The Light*. Originally, I had come up with the title of *Soul & Chips*, a clever play on words. But now that the book included contributors from some great luminaries, such as Don Miguel Ruiz and Neale Donald Walsch, I felt that the title no longer fit, and it needed the energy of a higher consciousness. *The Light* came to mind fairly quickly, but as usual I doubted this for several months until the time arrived when I needed to make a final decision. I had been reading Paramahsa Yoghanda's book, *Autobiography of a Yogi*, and feeling connected to him, so I asked him to give me a sign about calling my book *The Light*. I told him that I would open his book and that the first word I saw would give me the answer I sought. So I picked up his book, opened it up to a random page, glanced down, and the first word I saw was *Light*. This was a clear message, especially given the thousands of words in his book, not to mention those on just one page.

We all receive these signs and messages every day. Believe and be aware that everything that happens to you and the things you see may be Spirit's way of getting your attention or delivering a message you need in your life at that time. When you receive a message say thank you and then be open to other signs. The more you do this the more messages will show up.

The following stories are all amazing examples of receiving messages from Spirit. As you read the contributors' words, know that they are full of Truth and feel the energy behind the stories. In doing this you will open that invisible door leading to the world of Spirit and Light.

DAVID RATCLIFFE-FETERSTON
Psychic and Medium
Marbella, Spain

The Synchronicity of Spirit

This story tells of a period in my life from the age of 20 to 23 when one synchronistic event automatically led to another synchronistic event, which culminated in showing me how powerful and intelligent Spirit can be when we align ourselves to its presence. Even now when I look back at these events it still perplexes my logical mind how each "chance" encounter naturally led to the next, resulting in such an amazing outcome. It is almost like the unfolding of a story that you are not even aware you're telling until you arrive at its end.

At the age of 20, I was going through a very emotional period when every aspect of my life seemed complicated. I was feeling lost and unsure of my direction. I had recently broken up with my girlfriend, fallen out with my two best friends, and lost my job. I remember sitting in the house one evening when my dad asked if I wanted to join him at the local Spiritualist church in Northwich for that evening's demonstration. Back then my father was the vice president of the Spiritualist church so he attended most demonstrations. I decided to go along as I had no other plans. We arrived at the church and took our places at the back of the congregation. About halfway through the demonstration the medium approached us and relayed evidence of family members who had passed away. She continued speaking to me and providing counsel from my family members in spirit. They said that soon I would be moving away to work in Plymouth, South Devon. The medium added that whilst I was there I would begin to develop in mediumship as the spirit world wished to work with me. On the drive home that night my father and I discussed everything the medium had said. I could not believe I would be moving some 350 miles away to South Devon, as I had no desire to, and I didn't have any money.

Time passed and as the year progressed I found a new job. My life settled down for a short while and I celebrated my 21st birthday in Winsford with my family and friends. Later that year I found myself unemployed yet again, wondering where I wanted to go in life. My life in Winsford was becoming extremely depressing. I was unhappy with my job prospects and I felt like time was slipping away. I would often walk in the hills at twilight looking to the evening stars for guidance and help. I imagined that the North Star was my grandmother, and I would often voice my frustrations and ask questions to that star, and then listen intently for a reply.

One Saturday night in October, after a night out with my friends, I returned home to find that a family friend, Stephen, and his girlfriend, Clair, were visiting for the evening.

Stephen, Clair, and I chatted late into the night, and I eventually told Stephen my feelings about living in Winsford. Out of the blue, Stephen asked me if I wanted to move to Paignton. He said he could put me up in the building he was currently managing, and that if I wanted to go with them I had to be ready to leave by 8 a.m. the next morning. I knew I could not let this opportunity slip me by, as I had been asking Spirit to give me direction and help me find my purpose in life. Intuitively I knew this was the answer I had been seeking. So, taking a leap of faith and putting my trust in Spirit with only £50, my clothes, and my CD collection, I set out for a new beginning in South Devon.

I originally lived in a small room off one of the main halls in the run-down building that Stephen lived in and managed. The room had a bed, a wardrobe, a sink, no heating, and a cracked window. It was so cold in there at night that icicles hung from the inside of the window frames and I slept with two layers of clothes on and three duvets in order to stay warm. I had no money to buy real food and I found myself struggling to survive. Clair used to bring me any food left over from the chip shop where she worked every Sunday and Wednesday night, and those were the only nights when my hunger was satisfied. Stephen helped too, by allowing me to use his flat on the nights he stayed with Clair. On those nights I relished the hot showers and the heating.

I was determined to make a success of myself and I actively searched for work, but three months later I still hadn't found anything. During this time I often visited the library, where I could stay warm, and it was there that I found books on meditation and spirituality. I took them home with me and devoured their knowledge in those cold hours. I would sit, read, and then practice the meditation techniques. I found that I did not miss having a radio or television as I was so enchanted by my new discovery in spirituality. Even though it was a very trying period of my life I intuitively knew I was in the right place.

I went through the festive period alone and my New Year was celebrated with four slices of toast and a mug of tea. It was the first time I had been away from my family, and I felt isolated. I spoke with my mum in the New Year and she pleaded with me to come home. Although I was determined not to give up, I agreed that if I had not found a job by my birthday, on January 31, I would allow my dad to come and take me home. On January 25 I had an interview for a trainee manager's position in a supermarket in Paignton. On January 27 I was recalled for my second interview and offered the vacancy, which I immediately accepted. After that, I moved out of the cold room and into my own flat and began a new chapter of my life in Paignton.

My new employer told me that even though I would be working in Paignton, I first had to go to the shop in Plymouth to begin my training. As I sat on the train heading to Plymouth the medium's message returned to my mind. It shocked me so much that I began thinking about the spirit world even more.

Not long after, my mum visited and we decided to go to the Spiritualist church in Paignton. Again, I received communication from Spirit that they were aware of my recent hardships and that now was the time for me to unfold my spirituality fully.

The medium then went to a man who was sitting in front of us, gave him evidence of his family in Spirit, and confirmed that the student he had been seeking was sitting behind him. The medium pointed to me as he turned around and I realized that I had found my teacher. My development began just as the medium in Northwich had predicted. I did go and work in Plymouth and I did start to train in mediumship.

I loved living in my new flat but after rent and utility bills increases I struggled to make ends meet. I considered moving, but a few days later at lunch in the staff canteen I overheard a lady behind me talking about taking in a lodger at her home in Ellecombe, Torquay. One week later that lady was my new landlady. Not only did I now have better accommodation for less money, but I had also found a new job with better prospects, within walking distance of my new home. I felt truly blessed!

I settled into my new job as an assistant manager for a charity organization. I began recognizing the regular customers, and within no time formed a good rapport with them. One Friday in May I found myself unexpectedly managing the till as our volunteer for that day had phoned in sick. During that morning I saw lots of new faces but one man in particular stood out. He introduced himself as Paul, and, like me, he had recently moved to the area. We got talking about the FA cup final between Liverpool and Arsenal taking place the next day. As a fellow Liverpool supporter Paul invited me to join him and his friends at his local pub, the Ellecombe Arms, which I walked past every day.

Saturday came and I decided to stay home so I ordered the FA cup final over Pay Per View. At 2:30 p.m. the channel had still not unscrambled. I stood in the kitchen debating whether to take

Paul up on his offer when I clearly heard a voice saying, "Go out and enjoy yourself." I left the house and headed to the Ellecombe Arms. Three minutes later I was introduced to Paul's friends as we all prepared to watch the start of the match. At halftime I stood at the bar waiting to order my drink when Paul came over and began chatting with me. The conversation turned from football to where we used to live. I told him that I was from a small town called Winsford and Paul started to laugh because his best friend from school had moved to Winsford when he was a teenager and they had eventually lost touch with each other. He told me his best friend's name was Ronnie Langley. Then it was my turn to laugh, as Ronnie Langley was a very close friend of my father's and he lived three minutes away from my family home. As you can imagine, Paul was excited by this news and I promised that after the match I would ring my father and get Ronnie's telephone number. Paul asked me who my father was, so I told him "David Feterston." Paul's face seemed to freeze and he went pale as the color drained from his face. He asked me again, "What's his name?" I repeated, "David Feterston." Paul told me not to move and he dashed off, pushing his way through a crowd of people. I lost sight of him, thinking he was a little strange, and feeling confused at his reaction. Paul returned a couple of minutes later with a lady he introduced as his sister, Sharon. I told her how nice it was to meet her, and Paul said, "Tell Sharon your name." I did, and she replied, "Is your grandfather's name Bill?" I stood stock still, unable to understand how this stranger could know my grandfather's name. Eventually I confirmed that was my grandfather's name, and when I asked how she could possibly know, she replied, "Because he's our grandfather too." I stood there, stunned, not absorbing what she had just said. Again she repeated that Bill was their grandfather and that their mum's name was Patsy. I thought this was all a big prank. When Sharon and Paul assured me that this was no joke I rang my father and asked him if he had a sister named Patsy. My father was so stunned that I had to repeat the question. When he had recovered he confirmed that he did have a half-sister named Patsy and that he had lost touch with her many years ago. I went on to tell him that I was standing with Patsy's children in a pub in Ellecombe, South Devon, some 350 miles away from Winsford and Liverpool.

Because of the series of synchronistic events, my father and his siblings were reunited with their half-sister Patsy, whom they still see today. Paul was reunited with his long-lost friend Ronnie, and Paul was in fact my cousin, who introduced me to my other cousin, Sharon.

My father eventually told me the story of Patsy. Many years ago, a lady had knocked on my grandmother's front door and asked if William Feterston lived at this address, to which my grandmother confirmed he did and asked why she wanted to know. The lady stated, "Because he may be my father." The lady, known as Patricia, was invited into the house, where my grandfather confirmed that he was previously married under the name of William Fetherstone to Julia Kehoe and they had two children together, Patricia Fetherstone and William Fetherstone, Jr. After that marriage my grandfather had unofficially changed our family name to Feterston. Patricia had been searching for her father for many years before she finally found him. My father and his siblings were all called to the house to meet Patricia. Phone numbers and addresses were swapped and my father and Patricia stayed in touch for a number of years before communication was again lost. All of these events happened when I was a small child of around 5 so I never knew about any of it.

I never expected that a simple prediction from the medium many years before at Northwich Spiritualist church could take me on such a journey. Not only had I found a family that I never knew existed, but also the questions I had raised as I looked up at the north star a couple of years back had now been answered. I finally knew what my dharma was in life. I was to devote my life to the Truth that life continues after physical death and that Spirit is eternal.

ANGELA DENT
Retired Restaurant Owner
La Viñuela, Spain

My Grandmother

My first child, Daniel, was a little premature and needed feeding every three hours. This went on for some time and I was eventually exhausted. Daniel was born in October and my paternal grandmother passed away in November. I was very close to my grandmother. I was her first grandchild and I had been with her almost every day throughout my first few years of life. Back then, I was the light of her life and we remained close until she passed away. One night I heard my grandmother calling to me. "Angela, Angela," she called, "if you don't wake up you're going to kill your baby." I suddenly awoke and found that I had fallen asleep while feeding Daniel in my bed, and my body was covering his. Indeed, had I not awoken I would have smothered my baby.

JENNIFER MACKENZIE
Teacher, Lecturer, Clinical Hypnotherapist, Trance Medium, Healer
Marbella, Spain

Australia

One day I was told by Spirit to go to Australia. I didn't know anyone there, but I was given the name of a medium in Sydney. I was told to stay for a month in a studio apartment in a place called

Brighton. At this time my home was in Brighton, Sussex, in the UK, so it seemed strange that this is where I was being sent.

I arrived in Sydney when most things were closed, but I managed to share a taxi with a very nice lady who was also going to Brighton.

I arrived, booked into my room, and enjoyed Brighton for a couple of days. Once I had recovered from the journey I decided to do something about a studio. I asked the janitor of the hotel, who told me his brother ran the Post Office Tower just over the road. This seemed perfect; a high-rise block with stunning views. I went straight to reception. "No, we have nothing," said the man behind the desk. "Yes, you do," I said. This went on for some time until, exasperated, he went through the reception book for a third time. Spirit was right; someone had left a vacant studio that morning.

I settled in quickly, phoned the medium whose name I had been given, and then went to see her. I stopped on the way to pick up some flowers, but there were only wallflowers left in the shop as it was late in the day. I took them to my new friend, who opened the door and said, "My goodness, Jennifer, you have brought me wallflowers! Those were my husband's favorite. He died 10 years ago and today is our wedding anniversary."

The following morning I set out for a nearby school to facilitate some classes arranged by this lady. Before I left I made sure all the windows of the studio were shut and locked. The day was brilliant, the teaching went well, and I had more than 25 students.

I rushed home, and as I opened the door I shouted out, "Thank you, God, for my day!" There was a sound like a trumpet and all the candles in the apartment suddenly lit up in unison, even those that I had never lit before. And on the floor of the sitting room lay one very large white feather.

NATHALIE FRANKS
Hairdresser
London, United Kingdom

Ask and You Shall Receive

I remember standing on a hill and praying to God when I was 13 years old. My prayer was a rant: "If this is all there is [meaning what I could see going on in the physical world], then I don't want to be here, so please show me another way." I did not understand what I was asking for, although my true self, the part that has wisdom, knowledge, and compassion, knew exactly what I was seeking.

I left the hill and forgot about my request. Between the ages of 15 and 21 I searched for some meaning to my life and read books from all different perspectives. I felt a quality of "Light" when I would sit and pray in the synagogue, but I did not like the fact that religion had a separation factor. I was seeking an experience of Light that would be all-encompassing, beyond race, creed, color, circumstance, or environment.

My two turning points came when I read *Siddhartha* by Herman Hesse and *The Prophet* by Kalil Gibran. It was the first time I had a deep connection to anything I had read. Another experience of Light occurred when I sat in a circle in a Spiritualist church. I left my body, heard a great buzzing sound in my ears, and saw an old man with a long beard taking me across a golden bridge. When I came back into my body I was utterly confused and I asked the leader to explain what had just happened. She could not.

I loved to go clubbing, so at least three times a week I hung out in several different clubs. One night I met a guy called Jack who was quite an intense young man. He spoke about a man called John-Roger and some seminars of his that he had attended, and he invited me to come along. I took him up on his offer and went to a flat in St. John's Wood. As I entered the flat I noticed that people were sitting on the floor, in low lighting with lit candles. They said a short prayer and called in "the Light." Then an audio seminar was played. As I listened to John-Roger, I thought, "Wow, this dude sees life from the same perspective as I do." As I was leaving the seminar I heard a strong inner voice say, *"This is what you have been looking for. Look no further."*

I attended these seminars regularly and was advised to start doing spiritual exercises—a process of closing your eyes, looking into the Third Eye area between the eyebrows, and chanting ancient spiritual tones. I had many wonderful experiences when I did this, and once again the buzzing in my ears would come and go.

Six months later, I had the privilege of meeting John-Roger when he came to London. I asked him about the experience I had when I left my body and saw an old man walking me across a bridge. He told me that I was a bridge for the new age and that I would be bringing many people from the old consciousness into the New Age consciousness. I was told that the buzzing sound is the "Sound Current," an inner sound that connects us to the basis of all life. It is the audible stream of energy that comes from the Heart of God. The Sound Current is mentioned or studied in many religions. In the Christian Bible, it is referred to as "the Word." There is a yoga tradition that focuses on the Sound Current, called Shabda Yoga. In MSIA (Movement of Spiritual Inner Awareness), the sacred tones chanted in spiritual exercises are in harmony with the Sound Current of God.

The Sound Current is the true Self. When you are in the Sound Current, you may feel a vibration, a rhythm, a hum, or a tone. If you are with the Beloved, you don't need anything else because you're riding right in the center of the Sound Current and, like the center of the storm, it is quiet and calm.

Now, 41 years later, I am still facing life and its challenges. I also have a deep, rich inner life, which provides me with the balance and peace I need to continue.

Chapter 4:
Birds, Animals, and Other Creatures, Great and Small

*A*nimals are often used by Spirit as a way to send a message or impart useful information to help someone in his or her life. People refer to these animal signs as totems, and we often find a certain animal showing up regularly for a while, until that animal has served its purpose. Then we may start seeing another animal everywhere we go instead.

My totem is clearly the white butterfly. For the last three years I have seen white butterflies in the most auspicious of places—on handbags, in shop windows, on birthday cakes, in books, at the beach, and fluttering amidst flowers (as butterflies do). This flurry of white butterfly sightings began about six months after I started putting together *The Light*. The time came when the book cover needed finalizing and no matter what designer I went to, I felt disappointed with each and every one of their ideas. Feeling desperate and in need of a little help from above, I asked the Light to help before going to sleep one night. In the morning, while I was in the state between sleep and wakefulness, I marveled over a flutter of white butterflies that was flying about my awareness. As soon as I fully awoke, I smiled, knowing that a single white butterfly must grace the front of *The Light* book cover. From then on, whenever I wondered or worried about *The Light* and its progress, a white butterfly would turn up to put my mind at rest.

The following stories all reflect this core theme that animals speak to us and tell us what we need to know.

Angela Dent
Retired Restaurant Owner
La Viñuela, Spain

The Owl

My earliest memory comes from when I was 9 years old, when I was awakened by the sound of an owl sitting in the tree outside my bedroom window. It hooted for most of the night. In the morning a letter arrived from Italy bringing us news that my maternal grandfather had passed away. One evening many years later, while watching TV in the lounge, I heard the very loud hooting of an owl sitting in the tree outside. The hairs on my body stood on end and I said to my husband, "I'm afraid we have lost another member of our family or someone very close." Indeed, news that a member of our family had died arrived the next morning. The time of passing over was the exact same time as I had heard the owl. Throughout the years I have noticed a pattern: If the sound of the owl is very near, a member of the family or a very close friend has passed away. The further away the sound of the owl, the less close we are to that person. However, the one thing that is guaranteed is that an owl's hoot always brings me news of a death.

PAMELA GOLDSTEIN
Writer
Amherstburg, Ontario, Canada

On the Wings of a Prayer

I've always thought it strange how we forget major details when trying to recall a life-altering event, but something minute, such as what we ordered for dinner at a restaurant, remains vivid. For example, I had salmon almandine with roasted vegetables and an arugula salad on August 2, 1990. That was the day Saddam Hussein ordered his troops into Kuwait and took over the country. I do not recall the exact details of the attack, nor do I remember how many Kuwaitis were killed. I do remember feeling ill with dread and wishing I had not eaten the salmon.

"He'll go after Israel if anyone tries to stop him," said my Chaldean friend. "He's crazy and is fixated on destroying Israel and killing Jews." The moment those words left my friend's mouth, I knew they were true and Israel would be in trouble yet again, simply for existing. And all we could do was watch the events unfold on our televisions, unable to do anything to help our little country.

Several tactics were tried throughout the months to stop Saddam. International condemnation made him laugh. Economic sanctions seemed to make him buoyant. When the United States and Saudi Arabia formed the Coalition of the Gulf War, he chortled with glee. I prayed someone would give him serious doses of anti-psychotic medications to stop his grandiose delusions. Nobody did, and his "game of war" continued.

After the bombardment of his troops on January 17, Saddam announced to the world, "The great duel, the mother of all battles, has begun. The dawn of victory nears as this great showdown begins." Twenty-four hours later Iraq launched eight SCUD missiles into Israel. My husband and I may as well have been glued to our seats in front of our TV, because we stayed in them for hours. Klaxons blaring, smoke billowing from apartments in Tel Aviv, children crying...it was more than I could bear.

"Dear God, why?" I asked before I went to bed. I cried myself to sleep that night, my heart heavy with despair. The days of battle turned into weeks, and the missiles continued to fall on Israel. I was disconsolate. One awful night the klaxons blared while Benjamin Netanyahu explained what Israel was up against. She was surrounded by 21 Arab nations and very few of them even recognized Israel as a country, let alone as a friend.

The next morning, I awoke to the phone ringing. "Mrs. G., look out your window!" said my young neighbor, Brett. "It's the Rambo of all pigeons in our tree!" I quickly looked out and found not the Rambo of all pigeons, but rather a giant, silver-gray hawk. He stood more than three feet tall. When he slowly spread his wings I gasped. One wing spanned an easy four to five feet. Did such enormous hawks even exist? I certainly had never seen one as large as this!

"He has to be a Harrier to be that big," said my husband, Will, an avid bird-watcher. "What's he doing in the city?" I couldn't say a word because, at that moment, the hawk slowly turned his head almost one hundred and eighty degrees and stared right at me.

"Wow, he's got his eye on you," Will said. "That's kind of creepy."

I got dressed and went outside. The hawk never took his eyes off of me. He was magnificent. The color of his feathers was like nothing I had ever seen before. Shimmering, iridescent silver—even that didn't describe it. When the sun's rays graced their light on its wings, the feathers took on an ethereal glow. It was so bright, I had to shield my eyes.

His eyes never left mine. As I moved from room to room while cleaning my house, I'd look out the window and he'd be staring at me. I felt unsettled when we made eye contact. "Who are you?" I whispered. "Where did you come from?"

Five days passed since the hawk's arrival and the attacks on Israel continued. After missiles hit Israel yet again, I rushed to the window. The hawk remained in the tree at the back of my house staring at me.

He didn't move.

I spent my mornings sitting in a chair in my backyard, taking in every detail of this incredible creature. I flicked through the pages of every bird book I could find. My hawk was not in any of them. Birdwatchers came to the house and marveled at my hawk, but he only focused on me. He was here for me, but I didn't understand what he was trying to tell me.

As I drove home from work on the day before the Gulf War ended, the colors surrounding the setting sun changed into vibrant shades of green, mauve, and orange. I wasn't the only one who pulled my car to the side to observe this phenomenon.

"I ain't never seen nothing like that," said one man.

"I did, once," said an elderly gentleman. "We had just won the Big War. An incredible sight. Never thought I'd be blessed enough to see it again."

I drove home, breaking all the speed limits on the way, and then I ran into my backyard. The hawk was still there. He leaned closer and looked down at me. Those eyes that had kept me so unglued all week were no longer frightening.

A warm serenity seeped through my veins and I felt at peace. Everything was going to be okay. I smiled. "Thank you," I murmured. My hawk spread his beautiful wings and with one final glance at me, he flew away. And my spirit soared with him.

It was no shock to me when my husband announced the next day that the war had ended. "You don't seem surprised," he said.

"I'm not," I said, laughing.

Years have passed since the visit from my hawk and there have been many times when I have fretted and cried over what has happened to Israel and the world. So often I have felt as if we are on the brink of a man-made cataclysm that none of us will ever survive. And just when I feel the most despair, a hawk swoops down and sits in my tree. It's not a coincidence; it has happened too many times.

I am now amazed in these especially stressful days. Not only do I have hawks in my backyard, but there is also a pair of bald-headed eagles nesting nearby. We haven't seen eagles in my town for decades. People come from all over to see the town's nesting peregrine falcons. Other birds unknown to this region have also arrived, such as white-billed cuckoos, and a great gray owl. It was originally thought that the presence of these creatures was a fluke, but the cuckoos have been here now for three years running. Cranes have suddenly increased in numbers too.

Everyone has their own theory as to why this phenomenon keeps happening. Were these incredible creatures sent from God to remind us to have faith and trust in Him to do what is best, and know that everything will work out fine?

I heard on the news that Syria gave Hezbollah missiles and my heart began to flutter with panic. Another war? How will we survive? Those thoughts barely formulated in my mind when a large Harrier hawk flew by my window and landed on my roof. Another sign from God? I am certain the answer is yes!

DEBORAH JAYNE HAYES
Journey Practitioner, Doula, and Healer
Brighton, United Kingdom

From Tragedy to the Light

In July 2011 some of my friends and extended family members were killed in a motor accident on holiday in Jamaica.

I was visiting India for the first time, and my friends and I were at the airport ready to take a flight back to the UK. We missed the flight, so we booked a hotel for the evening, had a meal, and began to watch a movie. After the meal I received a phone call from my daughter, who was very distressed. "What has happened?" I asked, concerned. She couldn't speak for what felt like a lifetime. "What's up?" I asked again. Finally, she replied, "There has been an accident." Then she cried out seven names, followed by a primal cry from deep within.

The following day, on the flight home, I thought of my friends and family who had passed away in Jamaica, and how my girls were dealing with the grief.

I arrived back in the UK to discover that out of the seven friends in the crash, three of them had survived. Josie, my best friend's daughter, was in a coma in Jamaica. Josie's brother had survived with some injuries, and Josie's boyfriend was also okay. Josie's parents, sister, and best friend had all passed away. She would discover this devastating news when she awoke from the coma a few weeks later. Josie suffered from two broken legs, two broken arms, and a broken eye socket and jaw, along with severe brain damage to her frontal and temporal lobes. Considering all of this she is doing remarkably well, following her own healing path to recovery.

Josie's sister, Caisie, who had changed her name to Caisie Light, was just 17 years old, and was a beautiful, happy, bubbly girl who saw the love and joy in everything. She had wonderfully close friends, including my daughters. They had all known each other forever, and my girls were grieving and in shock about never seeing their friend's Light again.

I, along with close friends of those who had died, took Caisie's lifetime friends out to the river, where we remembered Caisie and the others who had passed away. It was a beautiful day and we did all the things that she would have loved: swimming and boating in the river, playing, and picnicking.

When it was time to leave, my daughter called me to one side and said, "I had a weird experience, Mum! When I went for a walk earlier three crows swooped into my path and flew about 100 yards in front of me. I know it was Josie's mum and dad, and Caisie!"

Josie's parents' earth animal had been the crow. Her dad was from a Welsh valley known as "The Valley of the Crows," and they had celebrated the crow for many years through music and art. This distinguished and highly intelligent bird is known as a great leader, just as were Josie's parents, who created platforms for great musicians and artists to show their work under the label Crow Zone.

After two nights of holding a space for all of Caisie's family and friends, I went home and placed my friend's pictures next to my bed. I then distracted myself on my computer, so as to not feel the grief.

Then something happened. Before I knew it, I was with Kath, one of my true soul sisters, the mother of Josie. I had the most amazing out of body experience, which I had never experienced before. As a practitioner of healing, this was the most profound spiritual experience I have ever had.

We were facing each other and no words were spoken. Kath telepathically told me that she was at peace now, not to worry, and to please take care of Josie, her daughter. I replied, "I will always be there for Josie!" Kath had a regal presence about her. She was shining the most amazing light from her wonderful, positive, beautiful soul. As we both bathed in the shimmering of a deep orange glow and the exquisite feeling of peace, love, and bliss, I knew all was well for those who had passed on.

As I became more comfortable, absorbing All That Is, I opened even deeper into this love. All of time and space had dissolved completely, so to this day I do not know how long I was there. Then, with no warning, I felt a kind of thud, as if my soul had popped back into my body. For a moment I didn't know where I was, and I didn't even recognize my own bedroom. I felt uncomfortably out of sorts. All I could think was, "Take me back."

Although it hurt to return to this reality, I am hugely thankful, humbled, and in deep reverence and gratitude to Kath, my Forever Soul Sister, who shared with me the most amazing experience I have ever had.

LAUREN SEBASTIAN
Creative Illustrator
La Herradura, Spain

As I entered the house for abandoned dogs and cats, I had no expectation whatsoever of falling in love. Life was great. I lived in a cute little house with my guitar-maker soul mate, and my "job" was to make art and illustrate pictures. We were a stone's throw from a beautiful beach in paradise, and, although we didn't yet have children, I felt no urgency. All in good time. I was visiting the shelter with an idea of becoming a volunteer, as I wanted to give something back to the local community. Then, I rounded the corner and encountered an assortment of delightful dogs—little ones, big ones, noisy ones, quiet ones. They had all suffered and now found themselves in the care of this wonderful place.

Sebastian was the tallest and most recent inhabitant. He had been found starving in the hills of Andalucía. A striking brindle Galgo (Spanish greyhound), and only one and a half years old, he was gentle and solemn. From the moment he saw me, he followed me, as I was given a tour of the complex. From the moment I saw him, to my utter surprise, I could not stop crying. I did not want a dog, yet I felt he *was* my dog and the thought of leaving him behind broke my heart. We decided to foster Sebastian.

Sebastian bore my family name, and I now realize that this was a huge clue from the Universe that I was about to do some Light-work on my genealogy. He was a guardian angel because, during those six weeks, I underwent a healing of my inner child that I hadn't even been aware I needed. Sebastian's presence and overt separation anxiety also uncovered layers of denial I had been holding inside, having to do with maternal instinct and responsibility. This unique and wonderful creature, whom I thought would be with us for the rest of his life, only stayed for six weeks. I knew that our home was not what he needed, as Galgos need space to run free and we didn't even have a garden. It took me all that time to let go of my desire to keep him, to release any feelings I had of inadequacy or failure as a "mother," and to fully comprehend that to really love him was to put his best interests at the heart of any decisions about his future. I had to do what was right for Sebastian and to honor his role in my life by ensuring he had the best possible home. He now lives very happily in Germany in a family with children and another dog. Sebastian provided me with an opportunity to experience authentic gratitude, which has now become a core part of my spiritual practice. I will always love him.

TERRY TILLMAN
Leadership Seminar Leader, Motivational Speaker Scout, Ketchum, Idaho, United States

Every year I take a group of people on a 10-day wilderness trip in the Sawtooth Mountains in Idaho. On the first day everyone chooses a buddy, and buddies are then required to know each other's whereabouts for the entirety of the trip. The idea is that everyone is safe and supported.

We assemble each morning after breakfast to discuss the day's activities. One morning someone said, "I haven't seen my buddy Bob for about half an hour. He went down to the river to wash his socks." So I said, "Well, we're about to start the day's activities, so go and get Bob." Ten minutes later this man returned alone and said Bob wasn't by the river.

More time passed and Bob still hadn't turned up, and we realized he was missing. We organized a search by grid so that everyone looked in a certain area, extending about a quarter of a mile outside the campsite. By now it was getting late and we had planned to spend the day rock climbing and doing a summit ascent in two groups. We knew that if we didn't set off, we wouldn't have time to finish the day. The guides and I decided to send the groups out, while the cook, Julie, and I would stay behind and continue searching until 1 o'clock. At this point it was 9 o'clock, and we were concerned that Bob was in trouble, and even worried that he had perhaps fallen into the river.

Julie said, "I'll go down by the river and you go away from the camp in the other direction and we'll keep checking back with each other." Midday came and we still hadn't found Bob. By now we only had an hour left to search. We had done everything logical and reasonable that we could think of. Up until now we had taken a strategic approach, and that hadn't worked, so I went inside and said, "I need help. Where's Bob?"

At that moment I heard a chipmunk chattering in the tree above me. I said inside, "Are you talking to me?" I heard, "Yes." So I said, "What do you want to tell me?" I heard, "Go down to the river." Even though my logic told me that was crazy, I did. I walked down to the river and heard another chipmunk telling me to cross the river. I came to a trail about 200 yards away from the river. I said, "Left or right?" I heard, "Left." I walked for five or 10 minutes and then said, "Are you still there?" The chattering got more intense and told me to turn left again. Between the trail and the river there was undergrowth, bushes, and fallen logs so I didn't think turning left was a sensible option, but I did as I was told, climbing through the brush and over logs, and returned to the river. And then there, right across the river, I saw Bob walking around. I yelled his name but he couldn't hear me over the sound of the rapids, and he started to walk away, up the stream. I threw sticks and rocks across the river to get his attention. Eventually he saw me. He couldn't hear me but I screamed at him not to move, communicating mostly with hand gestures. I went back downstream to the crossing log and then upstream. When I reached him he said that he was completely lost. I knew that. He had been wandering around a half mile away from the camp, and when I found him he had been walking in completely the wrong direction.

I said "thank you" to the chipmunk, and we continued the trip with everyone present and safe.

Chapter 5:
Seeing Spirit

Before my first experience seeing Spirit, I wondered whether I'd feel frightened if I unexpectedly saw a ghost or spirit in my house. When I did see Spirit for the first time, I felt anything but frightened. In fact, a sense of peace and calmness fell over me, like a warm, comfortable blanket. All I felt was Love.

Spirits generally vibrate at a much higher frequency than the density here on planet Earth. I've discovered that when I'm operating at a higher frequency for a prolonged period (through doing regular Light practices) I'm able to tune in to the world of Spirit far easier.

The first time I saw Spirit was in the middle of the night soon after I began having cellular healing sessions. I awoke suddenly, but felt trapped between two states—sleep and wakefulness. There was a loud ringing noise vibrating through my head and body, and I could barely move my limbs or torso. I managed to heave myself up onto the bed and rest back against the wall, and as I did so, to my left and about three meters away, I saw a huge orb of pure white Light hovering right there in my bedroom. It is a sight that I shall never forget as it was so surreal yet so real, both at the same time. Because of its vibration I knew that the orb of Light was male, despite having no physical form like us humans. I took a breath and then realized that the ball of Light was trying to tell me something—there was a strange sound emanating from him, like the sound a radio makes when it's not properly tuned into a par- ticular station. This battle between my head and heart continued and I knew that, had I been properly tuned in to the Spirit world, I would have heard what this orb wanted to tell me. It is no coin- cidence (as there aren't any) that the very next day I received the message to launch a book including the people who had helped me to awaken my own Light. That book later became *The Light*!

Since that night, I have seen Spirit on several more occasions, and each separate encounter filled me with Love, peace, knowing, and wisdom.

The stories in this category are all written by those who have seen Spirit in various forms. I find it fascinating how Spirit ap- pears to each of us a little differently, hoping we'll tell each other!

JENNIFER MACKENZIE
Teacher, Lecturer, Clinical Hypnotherapist, Trance Medium, Healer
Marbella, Spain

Seeing Guides in Solid Form

After having taught mediumship for several years, I noticed that quite a few of my students had seen Spirit in the form of either a loved one or a guide. I thought about it and ranted at the Spirit world, frustrated that these people could see yet I never had.

That night I was awakened by a bright, glowing light, and by my side sat the most beautiful man I have ever seen; blond hair to the shoulders, tanned skin, blue eyes, wearing what appeared to be a white toga garment, with white wings stretching from his back. I pinched myself to make sure I was not dreaming. This wonderful being smiled at me and said, "We are always with you. You do not need to see us but I have come in this form to prove it to you. Go on with your work and know that we are overshadowing you."

K.T. BRADLEY
Truck Driver
Milford, New Hampshire, United States

Seeing Spirit in Dream State

Curiosity leads us to exploration: some explore the highest peaks or farthest lands; some probe the depths of the ocean or the vastness of the heavens above us. Further still are those of us who explore deep into stardust, whilst others scour ancient texts in search of God.

I am an explorer of the mind and soul—specifically my own. The further I dig and the deeper I push, the more amazing are the findings. A long time ago I unearthed all of my own truths. I faced all my lies and demons. I tethered them and learned how to control and use them.

Once I had discovered my truths and found out who I was, I pondered, *What else is in here? There must be more...* I was right. Lucid dreaming was the first art I indulged in, opening the depths of my subconscious mind. But I found something else down there: enlightenment, and an awareness that there was much more to my existence.

My background is fairly ordinary. I grew up in New Hampshire with my loving family and went to Catholic Church, which I've since abandoned. However, I still follow the teachings of Jesus, as He stood for peace, love of God, and love for our brothers and sisters. My childhood was happy, so long as I was with my family. Outside of my family unit I was never really accepted, and to this day people seem to keep their distance even though there is no apparent outward reason. My family as a whole is normal, apart from my paternal grandmother who claimed to have visions and such like. Unfortunately, she died when I was young, long before my own enlightenment. Interestingly, looking at photos of her when she was much younger, I see myself, most notably the distant look in her eyes, as if she feels what's on the other side of the curtain.

Of the many experiences I have had, one in particular sticks in my mind due to the fact that all five (or six) senses were fully engaged. It began with a simple dream. I found myself in my maternal grandparents' home, which looked much like it had when I was a child.

The change in consciousness was abrupt. I knew my body was asleep in my bed, yet I was fully awake somewhere else, and I did not have the ability to manipulate the environment around me. I was drawn to the basement of the home, a friendly and familiar place. Worn red and white tiles checkered the floor in a unique pattern. There was old furniture and an upright piano—Grampy's pride and joy. I spent every Christmas Eve here throughout my childhood. The basement no longer exists in this form, as it was converted into an apartment, yet there I stood at the bottom of the stairs overlooking the space I know so well.

I approached a dull wooden door, which opened to Grampy's old workshop. Curious, I took the handle, yet it failed to turn despite being unlocked. Someone was on the other side holding the handle...someone who was surprised by my presence. I felt as if I wasn't supposed to be there. The initial resistance went away, and suddenly the knob turned freely. I entered the workshop, finding it just as I had remembered, woodworking tools neatly in their places, cardboard boxes on the floor filled with scraps and mistakes, unfinished projects here and there. Only now it all looked somehow different.

A warm, radiant light filled the space in a way that no shadow could find a corner or crevice to hide from it. The room was awash in light. The light did not blind me, though; it was pleasant and muted like a warm bath, wrapping around me in a warm current.

I blinked my eyes and saw him there, so familiar yet so different. "Grampy?" I said. He had passed over not long after my wedding some nine years ago. My mind caught up with my eyes, taking in the soft light all around him; he looked so young, so strong. His hair was dark and full, and his muscles were toned under the blemish-free skin of his right arm and shoulder, exposed by his white robe. The image was unreal. I had never seen him in his youth—perhaps in a photo or two, but never in such detail.

I took a step closer and his face melted into a careful smile. I am sure he wasn't expecting me. Although he did not speak aloud I somehow understood he would come to someone who needed him. He had thought it would be my grandmother. We were both caught off guard by this meeting.

We both figured it out at the same moment, as his smile faded and his arms opened. He knew how badly I was hurting at this time. He knew how depressed I had felt in the previous weeks and months. He had been sent to bring me hope and peace, and that's why I had been guided here by some unseen hand, probably the Lord Himself, or maybe my guardian angel. I didn't know, and in that moment, I didn't really care.

I opened my arms and fell into his. Despite being the same height as him, as we embraced I felt small in his arms. He felt so strong and vital, so pure and comforting, like no hug I had ever experienced before. The feeling of utmost peace and happiness enveloped me, every sense overwhelmed with the purity of his being. I felt everything good about him with none of the bad. I felt his perfect self.

As he squeezed me tight I knew our moment was about to end and I felt him carry me back to my body where I lay in bed. Although my eyes remained closed I was fully conscious for one brief moment as he leaned in close to whisper four words in my ear, "I love you, Timmy." Like only he could. Very few people called me by that name; even fewer spoke it with the love he did.

After the tickle left my ear I shot up out of bed, fumbling for the light, the torrent of emotion overwhelming me as I tried to make sense of what had just occurred. I have had a handful of intense experiences like this and each has left me sobbing uncontrollably. Love is the only way to articulate what I felt in that moment; limitless, pure love.

I have been gifted with these little peeks at what is beyond and I pray that God continues to grant me these insights until He comes for me. I will never fear death because for those of us who carry the light in our hearts, there will always be a place at God's side.

SHARON MAY SAUBOORAH
Psychic
Enfield, United Kingdom

Smile of a Stranger

When I was 5 years old my insistent statements that "I've seen a man in my room" were finally taken seriously. Often, when children have spiritual visions their visions are dismissed by adults as mere imagination. Parents assume that their children are giggling at absolutely nothing. What they don't see is the figure, spirit, or angel that is smiling and communicating with the child. This may sound unbelievable because as we grow into adulthood, we are mentally trained to only believe in the logical. My childhood experiences paved the way to a spiritual way of life, which has helped me to assist and guide others.

From as far back as I can remember I have always slept with a light on. In my childhood years it made me feel safe and secure, and it enabled me to see my room clearly. You see, for me the darkness held more than just shadows—it allowed the tall man to visit me. He was a frequent visitor and I would often see him standing at the bottom of my bed, completely silent but always smiling. On numerous occasions, I had tried to explain to my mother about these visits but my ranting was dismissed as childish imagination or dreaming. Then, one night, the visits changed, and for the first time ever, something physical happened.

On this particular night I had pulled the blankets over my head, leaving a small gap to breathe through. I didn't want to see anything or anyone, and I thought if my face was covered, I wouldn't be able to. This must have worried the man because he pulled the blankets off of my head and then stood there, looking concerned. This prompted me to call out to my mother. Hearing the urgency in my voice, she quickly ran upstairs and into my bedroom, my older sister close behind her. Whilst hugging my mum as tight as I could muster, I explained to them both what had happened. This time my experience was not dismissed as a dream or as my imagination. For the first time, my mum and sister listened to me.

My sister is 10 years older than me and she convinced Mum to listen to what I had to say. She asked me to describe the man I saw each night. With great relief I told them that he was tall and slim with black hair and a moustache. As I finished speaking, they both looked at each other in disbelief and confusion. My sister then scurried away but returned within minutes holding a large black album in her hands.

She placed the album onto my bed and opened it. Carefully, with trepidation, she turned the first page and asked me to look at the pictures inside. She told me to see if I could see the man's face. Page after page was turned until, all of a sudden, I saw the face of my visitor. Excited, I shouted out that the man in the photograph was indeed the man who always stood at the bottom of my bed.

My mother's eyes welled with tears. Even my sister looked shocked and upset, as they stared at the man I had pointed at. After a few minutes my mother sat down beside me and explained as best she could that this man was my real father. It must have been difficult to say this to a 5 year old, but I do remember her saying that he was in heaven. My father had been killed in a car crash when I was only 10 months old, and I had never seen a photograph of him, nor had I ever been told anything about him until that moment. This was because my mum had met a wonderful new man who had taken on the role of Dad.

Looking back to those days makes me smile because I was blessed to have two amazing men to call "Dad": one who conceived me and another who raised me. At the time, one was in Spirit and one was on Earth. I believe that my real father was visiting me to make sure I was okay, but also because love is our strongest emotion. The love within his soul connected him to mine, and it still does now!

JOSEPH ALEXANDER
Medium and Author
France

My Life's Journey with Spirit

At Age 4

One day when I was 4 years old I was playing in my bedroom when suddenly the whole room lit up and a beautiful lady appeared. If I were to try and describe her, the closest I could come would be to say that she looked like Cinderella, just after the Fairy Godmother had waved her wand and cloaked her in a sparkly, twinkly dress. The lady had golden locks that went down past her shoulders, and her dress kept changing color. Even at that age I thought, *Ooh, this lady is very pretty*. But it did not hit me that there was anything unusual about her.

Then the lady spoke to me, and I have never forgotten her words. She said, "I have been sent to tell you that the journey of your life will be sweet and sour, but you will always walk with us."

"You're very beautiful," I said. "Who are you?"

She replied, very sweetly, "For your purposes, I'm a mummy figure."

"But I have a mummy!" I said.

"One day you'll understand what I'm saying," she replied.

At that moment, my mother came into the room and asked me who I was talking to.

I pointed across the room and said, "I'm talking to the lady."

My mother flew off the handle and left the room, slamming the door behind her and leaving me feeling confused. The lady then continued speaking. "Soon you will be moving house," she said, "but Daddy won't be going with you." About six months later my adoptive parents divorced, and we did indeed move. The day we moved into the new house, I saw that there was a little boy standing at the top of the stairs. He looked at me and said, "*I* live here."

"No you don't," I said. "We live here now, so you'll have to go and live somewhere else." But the little boy remained. At that age I thought he was just a normal boy.

At Age 5

When I turned 5, I started school. On my very first day, walking home, I met an elderly couple. The man said, "Hello, Joseph." I didn't recognize him or his wife. He carried on speaking. "We're from the house next door to the one you've just moved into," he said. I noticed that he had a funny foot, and he was wearing one big shoe. The lady was very sweet. They told me their names were Jack and Elizabeth. I went home and said to Mum, "I met a man who lives next door, and his wife."

A few weeks later, the lady next door was talking to Mum. During their conversation, she told Mum she was a widow.

"But my son seems to think that a couple called Jack and Elizabeth lives at your place," Mum replied.

"Oh no, that was about 20 years ago," said the lady. "I took over the house when they died. They died within two months of each other."

Then my mum said, "Was there anything unusual about the man?"

"He was a lovely old man," said the lady, "but he had a club foot."

And so began my journey, seeing people that nobody else could see. Mum ordered me never to talk about them, or else I would be in big trouble. Nevertheless, the first chance I got, I would blurt out the messages that the "unseen" people had asked me to pass on. As a result, I was often locked in my room for days on end.

As an Older Child

When I was 11, a little girl named Lalla came to see me. "I'm a spirit girl," she said, "so I'm dead." That scared me, because at my local church we were taught never to talk to dead people. They said it was evil...satanic...the dark side. It took three or four months for my guide to get me back on course. "Are you dead too?" I asked him one day. "My physical body is, yes," he replied. "But I'm totally alive, just in a different way."

As the years passed, I became a bit more comfortable about talking to "dead people," because people would say things like, "What you've just told me, you couldn't possibly have known," and that gave me the confidence to know I wasn't schizophrenic. But I was never a confident young man. I was tall and lanky and I wore glasses. I certainly wasn't the Brad Pitt of the day. I lacked confidence in many ways, but inside of myself, as Joseph, I did have a kind of confidence because of my communication with the spirit world. As a boy I was always known as the "odd kid," and people would cross the road to avoid me. That in itself knocked my confidence. But—and this applies to everyone's life—we grow, life's journey continues, we see new things, and we develop our own ideas intertwined with what other people have told us.

As an Adult

As a young man it was my dream to be an astrophysicist, but that never came about. With hindsight, I now understand that I was gently being guided to help people by talking to them. That gave me a level of confidence that I hadn't had as a child. I realized that part of my life's journey was to talk about how the spirit world works, and how there is no difference between this world and the other, apart from the fact that the other world is on a higher plane where our spirituality can develop further. At one stage I naïvely thought that perhaps I should go into the church and become religious. That idea was soon squashed when my guides said, "Your journey is not about being in a closed world. You have to be in an open world."

I wondered where I should go from there. The obvious move was to become a teacher. After a while, however, that wasn't enough for me, so I decided to train and then work as a doctor. Then, in my 40s, I suddenly had a great urge to train as a child psychologist, and I did a five-year counselling course. With my experience of life, the help of my spirit friends, and by the grace of God, I did soon become a counsellor. At the age of 60, I decided to retire from professional life. I thought I could sit back and relax a little, but Spirit had other plans for me! That is when the great journey of my understanding of life truly began, and I traveled the world to give readings and lectures. By now I am well into my 90s, and I have traveled to 110 countries and have met thousands upon thousands of people.

One day, when I was 72, I walked to the local park. On the way there, I bought a school notebook and a couple of pencils. I sat down on a park bench, and soon an old lady walked past. She looked at me and said, "You're a writer, aren't you?"

"No," I replied, "but I used to be a teacher."

She said, "No, you're a writer." Then she walked away. I realized that the clothes she was dressed in belonged to the 19th century. She looked back and she smiled at me. I opened the notebook, and suddenly I got the urge to write. The words were focused on my life's journey. This ended up as my first book, *Talking with Spirit*. To my great surprise, it sold nationally and internationally within a year. I discovered that writing books is a good way to get the word out. By now I have written many—it's clearly a part of the plan for my life.

We should always remember that we are each a person in our own right. God has given each one of us special gifts, and he is there watching us and guiding us. Because of God's power and omnipotence, the knowledge that he is standing so close all the time could be a bit scary for people, and so, in his grace and pure love, he has given us angels from his Infinite Light to guide us. These guides and mentors are with us from the day we are born right up until we draw our last breath, and then they are there again to greet us in the next world. We need have no fear; the Light contains everything we need.

Chapter 6:
Jesus and the Masters

Some people have seen or spent time with Jesus. I cannot claim to have met Him yet myself, but I dream to one day see Him while I am still here on Earth. I have met other Light-filled spiritual teachers in the dream state, though.

The night after I attended a Siddha Yoga intensive I dreamt that the Indian guru Muktananda came and touched my head and my heart. He also touched the copy of *The Light* book that I was holding in my hands. The book had not been launched by this point but it was due to come out within the next month or two.

Another night, I dreamt about the Dalai Lama, who had come to protect me from some Nazis that were knocking on the door. I have no real idea about the meaning behind this dream, but it felt as if he was protecting me from something.

One night I received a message from a spiritual being called Bartholemew in meditation. That was a strange experience, as when I told a spiritually awake friend the next day what he had told me, she sighed and smiled, saying, "That's just the information I needed to hear today." She went on to divulge that Bartholemew was one of her teachers in the spirit world, and she had always had a close relationship with him.

As you read the stories in this section, see what Master appears or makes himself known in your awareness. The energy of the words will surely attract a fair few!

Brian Longhurst
Author of Seek ye First the Kingdom: One Man's Journey with the Living Jesus
Gloucester, United Kingdom

A Holy Encounter

Each night I would kneel at my bedside, praying for a personal awareness of Jesus. Then, on the 24th of January, 1967, after my nightly outpouring, I began to prepare for bed. As I stood in the middle of the room, suddenly He was there, in the corner, in the midst of an aura of golden, living sunlight, which radiated out from Him more than an arm's length in all directions. He was about three or four paces from me.

As I became aware of His presence He began to move toward me. He was above the floor a few inches, and He glided. The progress was relatively slow, certainly unhurried, but as He drew nearer, He began to speak. I *heard* Him with my ears; I *experienced* His speaking with my soul, with my heart. There was no part of my being that did not hear Him. And every part of me understood, with a total certainty, the meaning, at a *soul-knowing* level rather than an intellectual level, the true, mystical meaning of those words. The words that He spoke were, I discovered later, from Revelation chapter 3 vs. 20: "Behold, I stand at the door, and knock: if any man hear my voice, and open the door, I will come in to him, and will sup with him, and he with me."

I had not read or heard those words before, but at that moment they were a timeless part of my being and I knew exactly what they meant because His imparting to me of the words also imbued my mind with the meaning and understanding of them—*His* meaning of them. By the time He had finished speaking He was half an arm's length from me, face to face. His aura enveloped me, and the feeling of Love—of *agapé*—to my being was so intense, so powerful, so uplifting to my spirit that I felt as if my heart had grown to the size of a football and would burst from my chest cavity. This feeling of all-encompassing, all-inclusive Love was complete, permeating not just my body but my entire aura in an orgasm of the soul, a thousand times more intense than any such bodily experience. I was blinded by a waterfall of joyful, rapturous tears, and every part of me was alive, pulsating, electrified, yet at total peace.

His presence was visible in the midst of the light of His aura, which was brighter than the sun but did not hurt my eyes at all. With me now fully within His aura, He stopped. His eyes were radiating the all-knowing wisdom of the ages, and love: personal love as well as universal, unconditional Love. I *knew* He loved me personally, in a way and with a love that is utterly beyond any love I had ever known, heard about, or experienced in this world. He embraced the entirety of my being with every part of His being— with his total, limitless, all-enfolding love.

I was a quivering jelly. Not from fear (how could fear exist in such an exquisitely beautiful, magnificent encounter?) but from being overwhelmed by the flawlessness of His love. The moment of this embrace seemed to be timeless—eternal—but was probably five or 10 seconds of Earth-time. I still, some 47 years later, recall it as if it was yesterday. I remember reading at some later date, in the Book of Revelation, chapter 1 vs. 16, "...and his countenance was as the sun shineth in his strength," and saying to myself, *That is an exact and perfect description of his appearance.*

The manifestation gradually withdrew and disappeared from my sight, but the power and sense of his presence that was left with me—in me—lasted for at least an hour, probably two. I have never taken any form of hallucinogenic or consciousness-expanding drug, but I have no shred of doubt that this feeling was a "high" beyond any induced by such substances. I had to physically restrain myself from rushing—more like flying—upstairs, outside, onto the rooftops, and calling to the world, "He's REAL! He's *really* REAL!" even though by this time it was well after midnight.

Eventually I slept.

The next evening I rushed to my friend Olga's and told her of this wondrous event. She shared with me how, many years before, one of her spiritual guides known as "the Teacher" had taken her out of her body to a temple in the Realms of Light, where he had instructed her, in the presence of Jesus and others, in a ritual of solitary or near-solitary prayer attunement. This is a mechanism for training the mind of the participant in communing with the Mind of Christ. This procedure is termed the *Service of Mystical Communion with Christ* (SMCC).

From that day on, for well over 30 years, I practiced this devotional attunement ritual. Any who *truly* seek and *earnestly* desire to commune with the Mind of Christ and faithfully follow the SMCC devotional ritual will be helped to achieve that state of communion (common union). The objective is for the mind to eventually become so attuned that the ritual service becomes unnecessary for achieving this communion at any moment, in any circumstances.

In November 1967 I told Jesus that my commitment to following His guidance was absolute; that if celibacy was needful for this, so be it; I was willing. However, as I had as many red corpuscles coursing through my veins as the next man, if celibacy was *not* the order of the day, would he please bring me a life partner with whom to share this journey. I then left it with him and forgot about it. Four months later, under synchronistic circumstances that so nearly didn't happen, I met Theresa. She has now been my beloved wife for 45 years. A few days after we met, Jesus came to me as I was retiring for the night and said, "I have brought the little one to you to be your Companion of the Way."

TERRY TILLMAN
Leadership Seminar Leader, Motivational Speaker
Scout, Ketchum, Idaho, United States

When I was in my late 30s I experimented with nutrition and fasting. I had just finished a liver flush: for one week all I took into my body was citrus juice, garlic, olive oil, and cayenne pepper. It was a heightened experience, and in trainings I could see through physical objects and people. When I worked with participants on their issues I'd see the entire situation visually, and I knew what people were going to say before they said it. Then I met a Korean doctor and he said that every year he did a water fast for 40 days. I liked the sound of that and felt intrigued, wondering if I could live on water only for 40 days.

The doctor showed me an exercise to do, which involved lying on the floor and wriggling around like a fish. He said this would keep my energy flowing, connect me with spiritual energy, and keep me alive. I had been running 30 to 40 miles a week and he said I could continue that with no problem. During the first week I lost 20 pounds, and I grew weaker every day.

Somewhere around the seventh day, I found myself with Jesus. Initially, it was dreamlike but it lasted for two days, so it was clearly not a dream. I could go in and out of it. I'd go and fetch a drink of water, or get up to go to the bathroom, but I was constantly with Jesus. Most of the time we were walking side by side engaged in conversation. I assumed we were in Israel because we spent a lot of time walking along dirt roads. He wore a white robe and sandals, but He didn't look like the suffering Jesus with a crown of thorns on a cross that is portrayed in the Catholic Church. I remember His joyfulness and His fantastic sense of humor.

For two whole days I asked Him questions and He gave me answers. I don't specifically remember the questions, but I do recall that the answers were clear, simple, and full of Truth....wise words and awareness, such as:

You are a creator. We create, promote, and allow everything in our life.

Clarity shows up along the way, never ahead of time.

The pauses are as important as the action.

Sometimes easy is hard.

Choose what you have and then you'll have what you choose.

There is nothing loving can't heal.

Where you look is where you go.

You can always choose your attitude at any moment.

What you think is real is determined by what you believe. With gratitude you are always abundant.

Sometimes you need to be silent to be heard.

To see clearly you need to close your eyes.

The ends and the means are the same. The way out is in.

There are no mistakes or failures, only experiences. What you do with those experiences is your choice. And that choice then determines your experience.

We only truly get what we want when we stop wanting it. (Wanting comes from not having, which is lack. Like attracts like and the energy of lack will attract more lack, not having...)

The less I possess the more I have.

Our body, emotions, and mind grow by receiving, taking in, getting. Our soul and heart grow by giving.

If you want more, give more. The Universe doesn't give. It gives back.

Learn to trust your intuition. It is your spirit whispering directions.

There is a blessing in everything. Ask, "What if this is for me?"

I can never have something until I let it go (until then, it has me).

The journey is the destination, after all.

Somehow all these Truths were implanted into me. The most common feedback I hear from those who attend my seminars and trainings is that I'm wise, and I know that shift into wisdom came after spending this time with Jesus.

I don't consider this a religious experience at all. It was a Spiritual one. My time with Jesus lasted for two full days and then I got up and passed out on the floor. At that point I stopped the water fast.

After that, I felt very different, and I have ever since. Meeting Jesus was a definite marker in my life. Since then I know at a deeper level who I am; I know who we are; I know that we don't die, and I'm not afraid of passing on. I know that it's all good, and if I don't, I recognize that I'm looking from too low a level of consciousness. Now it's easy for me to look at someone and see who they are.

I can even see the good in people whom I don't necessarily choose to be around.

SANDRA NICOLE CONCEPCION
Channel and Author
Philadelphia, Pennsylvania, United States

Note: *The following story is an excerpt from the book* Pink Roses for the Ill: A True Life Story of Severe Illness, Near Death Experience, and Conversations with Jesus and the Divine.

The feeling got stronger as the symptoms raged on. This was it: the hour of my death. The pull felt so strong. I had already accepted it, waiting like a child in front of a candy store before it opened for the day. Every couple of breaths required more effort than those I had taken in previous minutes. My body rattled. I felt myself peeling away from my own self, as I had done before in my sleep, but this time it was different as I was fully awake. *Here it is; here it comes: a universal moment that everyone eventually faces but that each must do alone. Death, as intimate as the birthing process, is imminent.* It is a mystery to us all until the moment we experience it. There are no words to describe the fear I felt within. There is no earthly event to compare to the sheer terror of death. All my strength and focus was channeled into letting it come and take me to the other side, wherever that was. A new fear added to the huge mound already in place: was I heading to hell?

My throbbing eyes needed to open, as keeping them closed for a long time sent pain piercing through my lids. My stare fixed on the mirror, telling me the time backwards from the cable box above the television. I did not want to watch each stretched moment pass. I didn't want my eyes to be open as I died.

As I began to close them, they sprang open again as the sound of chanting filled the entire living room. I lifted my head barely an inch and saw a blur of red and gold. As the blur neared me, I saw the faces of three monks in the mirror and in my mind's eye. Their robes and faces came into view. One of the older monks held a golden gong with a golden rod. He sounded the gong and I resisted the automatic urge to cover my left ear. I slumped back onto my stack of pillows, relying on my mind's eye to relay the event, instead of the mirror. The effort of holding my head up, let alone sitting up, was too much to bear.

The younger monk moved from his central position as the other two remained still. He lifted his arms and hovered his hands an inch or two above my head and neck. The second monk came over and did the same with his hands, palms face down over my torso. The gong and rod disappeared as the third monk came and hovered his hands over my legs. The young monk began speaking, reciting something in an unfamiliar language. The other two repeated these words, and then they recited them in unison. At this moment, chanting began. Their hands still hovering over my body, they chanted for a few moments until the young one lowered his hand, shortly followed by the others. Then the gong reappeared and the third monk sounded it. They all stepped back in unison, away from my body. The sound of the gong filled the silent air again, and it disappeared. They turned to the right and walked in unified formation towards my front door before vanishing completely.

Again, only the sounds of my own breathing and upright fan were audible. Impatiently, I waited for death to arrive, my breathing now shallower and quicker than before. *How long is this going to take? Why does it have to drag out like this?*

My ears picked up a dull drumming sound. I used the last of my physical strength to lift my head a few inches. From the direction of the dining room, a headdress of feathers trailing all the way to the floor entered the room. The headdress floated in the air, and then a man's face appeared under it, with wrinkled, dark brown skin. He wore a wide, beaded throat collar, which went from his Adam's apple to the middle of his chest. Layered hides of various browns and grays draped his shoulders, gathering at his waist. The same material covered his feet. A drummer and ceremonial dancer followed his appearance, and the three of them began a rhythmic dance with calls, yelps, and song, as though it had been rehearsed.

Not one of them spoke as they approached me. They continued their ceremonial dance and I sank back down on my pillow to watch: the drumming and the calling felt so good, like home. Tears fell down my right cheek into my ear. It felt orgasmic, as I let go of the reality of my death. Smoke and incense filled the air. I have smelled such scents before, yet not during this lifetime. These earthy smells overpowered me and I begged them to take me home to their land—my land. They did not respond.

The Chief stood over my head and neck, and he lifted his arms in the air to reveal a long, slender pipe and a white object that looked similar to a soup ladle. The Chief held the ladle over my head and tilted it slightly, and then he traced the outline of my body with it. Endless liquid came from the ladle's cup and fell over me. It burned at first and then it numbed my entire body. He directed the ladle all the way to my feet before lifting it high again. As the ladle disappeared, he took the pipe in his right hand and returned to my head. He leaned over and put the cupped pipe in my mouth for several seconds. I started coughing and he brought the pipe back to my mouth and throat. Great pain swelled in the middle of my throat. He held the pipe steady despite my resistance. Then he removed the pipe and stood upright once again. The ceremonial drumming and dancing stopped. The Chief, the drummer, and the dancer looked at me with their dark brown eyes. Each turned to his right, walked forward, and vanished one by one. My heart sank deeper as each of them exited. My tears turned into full-blown sobs as the room fell silent again.

I had little strength left. My lungs strained with each breath. The monks and the Indians had left me. Was I supposed to go with them? I had never felt so alone.

I saw movement out of the corner of my left eye. Grunting, I pushed up to see what little I could through the one-inch distance between my head and the pillows. Two things that looked like heads with unformed faces rose in the middle of my living room. Several feet from each other, they rose higher and higher, like hot air balloons lifting off the ground. Immediately, I began crying again. *This is it*, I thought. *They are coming to get me, and they aren't beautiful or magnificent. I have really screwed this one up. My fear is coming true! I am headed to hell for eternity and I will never see my family again.*

I slumped back in utter terror as I saw the heads rise higher through the mirror. I shut my eyes, sobbing harder, as I could see them in my mind's eye too. The heads stopped at my ceiling and two more formed behind them. Then two more appeared behind the second heads, until there were a total of 10. All of the heads hovered in a pyramid formation. I cried aloud, feeling terrified about what was coming to get me. I shook back and forth in an unsuccessful attempt to get up and run away. There was nothing left to do in protest; all my limbs were locked and my body was using a great amount of energy simply to breathe. I began to panic even more, screaming as loud as I could, both aloud and in my mind's eye. This was worse than any experience I had ever had. I felt my underwear grow moist. Surely a bowel movement would come next.

Suddenly a blinding white Light filled every corner of the living room, much brighter than any sunny day on Earth. I opened my eyes, squinting, and saw that the heads now had beautiful, innocent faces. The first being had short, wavy blond hair and stood in a gown nearly as bright as the light behind it. To the right stood a male being with long, straight brown hair ending at his upper chest. He too had a gown nearly as bright as the white light behind him, and with both hands he held a sword, the point facing downward. I felt my bottom jaw drop open and my eyes widen as I watched their every move.

"Do not be afraid," a voice boomed through my ears, coming from the direction of the blond entity. His voice deepened my fear, reaching a now unbelievable level. A sudden knowing came over me as the same entity showed me an animal stable. The view was from above, and there were several animals inside and two people fussing over a trough-like vessel. The vessel was filled with coarse hay and ripped remnants of cloth. In the center was a naked newborn boy, looking in my direction. I panted harder as the vision retracted.

Archangel Gabriel, could it be?

"Yes," the voice said telepathically. "It is I."

The same one who spoke to Mary and Joseph, and the Wise Men?

"Yes, Sandra, it is I," answered the voice.

My eyes were fixed on the mirror, in disbelief and fear. *Never have I seen a real Angel before, and now there is not one, but 10! They must be about eight or nine feet tall! Look at those heads and those hands!* "I am Archangel Michael," said the tallest entity. My eyes were drawn to his handsome face. He looked to be in his 20s or 30s, if measured in Earth years. He had a broad stance and a commanding voice.

Suddenly, a bundle of immense, supercharged energy formed in the center of this Angel pyramid formation. The new energy entity stood before me. He had light brown hair caressing his shoulders, yet at the crown of this head there was gleaming white. A defined beard from ear to ear adorned an olive-brown face. A white robe, covering the apparent torso and arms, was softly pinched at the waist with golden ropes and tassels. Olive-brown hands peeked out at the end of each sleeve; both arms were held widely apart from each other. His feet were covered in simple strapped sandals. I instantly recognized this entity, radiant in all His Glory. He appeared similar to all the contradicting depictions I've seen. Despite each variation, He could not be mistaken, missed, or unidentified. This entity was Jesus of Nazareth, Son of God and Blessed Mother Mary; the Savior, the King of Kings, the Man who died for every person's sins more than 2,000 years ago. This very Man was stood before me in my small living room as I reached my death. *It's Him; it's really Him!* Instantly, humbled respect filled me, as I mentally bowed before Him.

"No wonder you have trouble; there's not enough of Me in here!" Jesus stated with a smile. My thoughts went to the two crosses on my television stand, which have been there for months, possibly years, awaiting strong nails to be hammered into the wall for hanging. Our cross collection was also there, as we had not yet had them blessed. "My symbol is enough," Jesus replied to my thoughts. "It is man's belief that they need to be blessed." I tried to control my thoughts and hide them, but it was futile. He knew exactly what I was thinking before every thought manifested.

He came closer to me and I shuddered. His brilliant blue eyes pierced my entire mind. He could feel and see my soul. A forceful rush of shame and guilt unleashed itself. Never before had I felt so ashamed. I cried out, as the overwhelming sensation filled every crevice of my body and soul.

"You have forsaken Me," He said.

I have no idea what I have done wrong, Jesus, but please, please forgive me for all of it. I am sure there are many things I have done wrong, none of which my mind can recall.

He smiled. "My child," He whispered as He placed His right hand on my head. My head and entire body vibrated with powerful waves as if I had been struck by lightning. He immediately put me at ease. I willingly and happily surrendered to His touch, His supreme kindness, His omnipotent compassion, His amazing and perfect love. There is no feeling like it on this Earth; it is not of the material world. It was more than the love I have for my daughter and husband. His love surpasses all love. It is beyond unconditional; it is perfect and pure. Nothing could have prepared me to receive this level of kindness, compassion, and love.

The Angels continued to stand in silent formation, as Jesus held His hands high over my body, dropping His palms inches from me. He took His right hand and, like a scanner, slowly passed it over my exposed left side.

When are you taking me, Jesus?

"My child, you are not going to die now," He said. I became incredibly disappointed that I was going to live. I really felt death pull me in. "You have experienced what it is like to be terminally ill," he said, "right up to the second of death, except you didn't die."

Jesus, I want to go with you so badly. Why can't I go with you?

"Sandra, I need you to be my messenger," Jesus answered. "I want you to write about your experience so that others will understand exactly what an ill person faces in the process of dying, and what happens in the moments before their death. Generally when people are so ill, they do not get better and are unable to share their experiences."

I listened to Jesus's directions, despite my disbelief that I would stay alive and write about my experiences.

What do I do once the writings are finished?

"Sell it," He said. I used to write quite a bit, but lately not often. I was labeled as an unpublished novice writer. "It will be 50/50. I want you to give 50 percent of the earnings from the book you write to those who are terminally ill or seriously ill." He showed me a child with the St. Jude hospital symbol as an example.

Only children?

"No, all those who are ill," Jesus corrected me.

Why not 100 percent?

"You need to sustain your family's personal needs," Jesus answered.

I accepted the directions, amidst my doubt in being able to complete the described project. Even if I were to get well enough to sit up and type, would I be able to describe what had been happening to me for all this time? Would I be able to do justice to what I had just experienced with this visit from the Divine and this amazing conversation with Jesus, the Son of God? Why me? Out of all the seasoned writers in this world, why would He choose a novice writer to write such a story? And who will believe it, even though every event truly did happen? To my surprise, even I had trouble believing that Jesus and His Angels were really with me in my humble living room.

I will do Your will, I thought, setting aside all doubts.

Jesus laid His hand once again on my head. How I loved it when He did that. I pushed my head closer to His hand, and soaked in the moment. He gave me a knowing that He had set up a place for me in Heaven, but it was not the time for me to join Him. He had come to stop me from dying. He said I have a mission to accomplish and a lifetime of work ahead of me, according to His will.

"Do not worry and do not be upset that you cannot come with Me now," Jesus said. He told me that I had received healings from masters today and that death had been eliminated as a possibility.

Will you come again? Please don't leave me!

"Yes, Sandra, I will. I may be out of sight but I will never leave you," He answered.

I then felt ridiculous asking, as if I already knew this.

Jesus smiled and stepped back into the Angel formation. He hovered in that blinding white light, now oval-shaped, before vanishing into it. One by one the Angels vanished as well, starting first with the last that had initially appeared. Then, Archangel Gabriel disappeared and Archangel Michael immediately followed.

RICHARD WATERBORN

Cellular Healer
Cork, Ireland

There he was again, that "Indian guy," as I'd come to think of him, staring out from the photograph with those intense dark eyes, compelling my attention despite producing distinctly uncomfortable feelings in me, which I could neither understand nor name. It was Saturday morning during a residential weekend workshop on rebirthing, and we were seated in a circle on the floor of a large room, introducing ourselves.

I had stumbled across this remarkable process called rebirthing a few months earlier at a workshop pulled together on the spur of the moment by a colleague in the environmental organization we had set up. Our first major campaign—to outlaw the dumping of nuclear waste into the oceans—had brought us into close contact with Peter, the scientific advocate for Greenpeace, and we had arranged a meeting between him and the minister for the environment in Dublin. Peter had arrived shaven-headed, fresh from a lengthy stay at a remote ashram in the Himalayas, and once the meeting had concluded he was far more interested and excited to talk to us about his experiences in India, and to share a powerful healing technique he had learned there.

Though deeply unhappy and unfulfilled in my life, I wasn't actively looking for healing or interested in exploring myself, so it was more out of curiosity and respect for Peter's scientific credentials that I turned up for the impromptu workshop a few days later. I arrived expecting to learn something; to gain more information to expand my understanding of human beings, rather than be personally altered. I was wrong!

A crackling log fire warmed the chilly air of the converted old schoolroom, adding its radiance to the thin March sunshine streaming through the large windows. In one corner was a small altar upon which was a photograph of a young Indian man with strange markings painted on his face in red and yellow pigment. Peter introduced him as Babaji (a familiar Hindi word meaning "holy father") and explained that he was a Mahavata: an immortal master, and an incarnation of Lord Shiva, who could come and go at will between the physical and spiritual worlds. He would incarnate at times of spiritual ignorance and darkness to guide humanity back onto the path of the *sanatana dharma*, the universal spiritual Truth that underlies all religions. His most recent physical manifestation had been in a remote cave in the high Himalayas where he appeared as a youth of about 18 years old and remained in silent meditation without eating or drinking for 40 days. He taught *karma yoga*: union through devotion and service, and the use of the mantra "Om namah Shivai": I surrender to Shiva (God). Every morning at dawn he performed a sacred fire ceremony in honor of the Divine Mother.

As I listened I was mentally rejecting the story as irrelevant, impatient to get on with "the workshop," and to let the learning begin! I felt skeptical about Asian gurus, and protective about the inner relationship I had come to have with Jesus—not in the conventional religious sense, but through a number of very powerful inner meetings and revelations. What could I possibly want with some "foreign guru?"

That weekend changed the course of my life and launched me on a journey of self-discovery. Now here I was again, about to take another step on that journey, and there once again was Babaji's picture on an altar, those eyes staring into my soul.

This time there were two facilitators. Peter had been joined by a woman called Suma who had also been at Hedekhan with Babaji. She exuded a quiet inner strength and was a dynamic and effective facilitator whose direct and insightful feedback gave no quarter to fragile egos. As the day wore on I was feeling increasingly lost and desperate: nothing I was saying or doing was making me feel any better; on the contrary, the more I tried to elicit approval and recognition, the more rejected and unappreciated I felt, and I was consumed by a raw, livid pain, growing more intense by the minute.

At the same time—and to my own considerable bafflement—I found myself gravitating towards the altar in the corner of the room, and to the picture of Babaji. Almost furtively I began to tend it, lighting fresh incense and candles, cleaning away dust and ash. So new and strange to me was this behavior that it felt like it was directed by someone else who had temporarily assumed control of my body and nervous system. Yet this alien force felt comforting and consoling—so much so that during breaks when everyone had left the room I found myself lingering by the altar.

That night I lay wide awake in the dormitory upstairs, tormented by emotional anguish, which had become so unbearable that not even sleep would grant me relief. Tossing and turning, trying to physically escape from the pain that was gnawing at my insides, I eventually decided to get up and go home. Just at that moment, as I was getting up off the bed, I heard a voice say, "Turn to me." It was so clear and present that I looked sharply around in the semi-darkness for whomever had spoken, but even as I did so I knew with intuitive certainty that it had come from the same presence that lay behind the piercing eyes of the image on the altar downstairs. Drawn, as if by magnetism, towards this source, I dressed and made my way downstairs. The room was in darkness, save for a candle still alight on the altar revealing Babaji's face in flickering light and shadow. In the darkness the consoling presence was much stronger than it had been during the day.

As if in a trance, responding to some ancient and deeply encoded memory, I prostrated myself in front of the altar, forehead pressed to the floor, and I uttered the words "Om nama Shivai." A huge surge of energy coursed through my body like liquid light: a wave of sweet, all-embracing, unconditional love that flooded every cell of my body. Deep sobs racked my chest and tears poured from my eyes as my heart burst open and the anguish, pain, and grief of a lifetime, possibly many lifetimes, were engulfed and released just as a tidal wave uproots and carries away all obstacles in its path. The dark, fearull void of separation—from Source, from Mother, from Self—was illuminated and transformed into the ecstatic joy and gratitude of reconnection, of Oneness. I remained there, immersed in blissful contemplation for what seemed an eternity (though in "real" time it was probably less than an hour) before returning to my bed and falling into a deep, peaceful sleep.

So began a long journey of initiation, during which I came to realize the truth of Babaji's own words: that He and Jesus were One, from the same place, and that there are no religious distinctions or cultural boundaries within Godhead or between its avatars. Although Babaji had already left his physical body, I had several profound meetings with him on the astral plane. His teachings were always simple and direct, going straight to the heart, and his message was always the same: "Love and serve." During his incarnate life he had no desire to attract disciples or followers, and rejected any attempted devotion to himself, instead deflecting it to the Highest Source attainable: the Divine Mother.

In my last personal encounter, I was waiting in a long line of devotees to receive "darshan" from him. I had heard that looking into Babaji's eyes was like looking into the depths of the Universe, where everything was revealed. I was so excited I could hardly contain myself, or the love and gratitude I felt for him. I was carrying a gift, the most precious thing I could bring him. It represented me, my heart. When the great moment came, and I stood face to face before him, he looked deeply into my eyes as he accepted the gift. Then he gave a broad, warm smile and flung the gift up in the air where it shattered into a thousand pieces and dispersed among the waiting throng. At first I was dumbstruck, devastated at having my precious gift so ungratefully cast away. I looked back at him, and he was still holding my gaze, smiling. Then I got it. There was nothing I could give him, as he already had everything within himself. In taking the gift of my heart and giving it out to the masses of people around us, he showed me that the only gift worthy of him was my loving service to humanity.

VICTOR ARENCIBIA
Teacher and Author
Branchburg, New Jersey, United States

A Merging of Light

On a sunny autumn afternoon, on November 7, 1996, I went upstairs to do my daily meditation. On this day, I happened to remember an old audio cassette of ancient Aztec music that had been gifted to me several years before by a good friend. Interestingly, this cassette was still in its original plastic covering, unopened and unheard. I took the cassette, opened it up, and placed it into my Walkman (these were the days before iPods and digital music!). I sat down in my favorite meditation chair and got comfortable. I took a moment to do an invocation that I refer to as "calling in the Light," which went something like this:

> *Dear God, please be with me as I journey into this meditation. May all that takes place be for my soul's betterment. I ask for your Divine Light to be sent ahead to prepare the way for my learning and growth. I ask that any Divine experiences that may come about as a result of this day's meditation be so. Thank you.*

With that done, I began to listen to the music, which was different from anything I had ever heard. I focused on my breathing and, within minutes, I was out of my body. While I was still aware of my physical body's presence and location at home, I found myself flying over dark jungles somewhere in Mexico or South America. Flying, I could feel the cold wind on my face as if I were a bird. I flew for several moments, stopped, and then hovered high above a circular clearing in the jungle with a fire burning in the center. I glanced down and noticed a man dressed in white kneeling before the fire. As I descended, I realized that the man dressed in white was me.

I continued descending until I merged with his body. I was now consciously in front of the fire, literally feeling and experiencing its warmth. The night was still and quiet, almost too still. I looked at my body, glowing with white light.

I remained motionless for some time, when from within the jungle, beyond the fire, emerged two single-file lines. One line was led by Buddha, and the other by Jesus Christ. The line led by Buddha came around to my left and the line led by Jesus came around to my right. The two lines approached me and, one by one, each master merged into my body through the heart chakra. The lines continued merging inside of me in an alternating process. There were hundreds of different teachers and masters, both female and male, from every religion and beyond. This process continued until all became quiet and still once again. A moment later, out of the darkness appeared all kinds of animals, and the merging process began once again. There were tigers, lions, snakes, bears, birds, deer, and many more creatures. Eventually, the merging of animals ended and all fell quiet and still again.

Gazing into the fire, I noticed a slightly purple mist surrounding the clearing. Out of that darkness, Jesus appeared once again. He came toward me and stood to my right. Very sweetly and gently, He gazed down upon me and, without a word, He extended His left hand. I reached up with my right hand and placed it into His. He helped to my feet. In silence, we walked past the fire hand in hand, out of the clearing and into the jungle. Entering the jungle, I felt at peace. However, that peace would soon be challenged...

As we walked along a narrow path, I noticed that the hundreds of masters I had previously merged with lined the path on both sides, smiling. We walked for several hundred feet until the path ended to a cave opening. At this moment, I was placed high above the cave entrance facing all the smiling masters. Instinctively, I knew I was experiencing something special.

I was helped down and Jesus took my hand once again. We entered the cave, which had passageways lit by torches. As we walked, I noticed that the passageways steadily declined. We walked for a long time until the path ended, and we happened upon a cliff that dropped into a canyon several hundred feet down. I looked across to the other side of the canyon, which appeared to be approximately a hundred feet to the other side.

As we stood before the canyon, Jesus nonverbally told me that we would now walk to the other side of this canyon. Fear and panic overcame me. *There is no way I can walk on air to the other side*, I thought. *I will surely fall to my death.* Jesus smiled and said one simple word: *trust.* I knew there was no turning back, and with that, we stepped out, still hand in hand, into what I was sure would be certain death. I took a breath, stepped out, and instead of finding death, I found everlasting life. Sure enough, I did not fall. In pure wonderment, I watched myself walk across the canyon still holding Jesus's hand. The feeling resembled walking on an invisible, hard mattress. There was a bounce to each step. I clearly remember looking down past my feet, hundreds of feet below, in complete awe.

We arrived at the other side several moments later and stood before an entrance to another cave. We entered a room with a large wooden table around which sat seven very bright beings. I call them beings because they each shone a white light so bright that I could not make out what they looked like. At that moment, Jesus released my hand and stepped away, and the seven beings simultaneously turned to me and shot a white beam of light into my chest. An instant later, I was back in my physical body with my eyes open. The only words that came out my mouth were, "Thank you."

The music had ended. My body was warm and vibrating, and I felt a little lightheaded. I remember sitting in that chair feeling peace and joy. The warmth and vibrating continued for several days. I felt that I had become one with all of God's Divine messengers and living creatures. But the greatest gift from the experience was becoming one with the Christ that dwells within me. It was an experience of expansiveness and learning that would prove to be one of many such adventures.

Chapter 7:
Protected by Spirits and Angels

Several years ago, when I owned and ran a magazine in Spain, my dad would sometimes come with me to help deliver and distribute the magazines to local businesses. Part of the journey involved driving up to a place called Lake Viñuela, a popular area for relocating expats who had moved to Spain looking for a better way of life.

Halfway up the mountain, the road changed to two lanes, so that cars could overtake slow lorries chugging alone in the right-hand lane. However, on the other side of the road, there was only one lane. I'd recently purchased a new car, so, feeling courageous, I went into the left lane when I could, to pass slow-moving traffic on the right.

However, a lunatic driver coming the other way had also passed into my lane to overtake a slow car on his side of the road, where there was only one lane. My dad and I both shrieked as we saw this car coming straight towards us at a high speed—bracing ourselves for a head-on collision, and almost certain death. I felt frozen with fear, but something came over me and I suddenly moved the steering wheel swiftly to the right to get back into the right-hand lane, without even looking to see if there were cars. It felt as though something—a higher power—had taken over to ensure the safety of my dad and I. Luckily, there was a gap in the traffic so no one was harmed and there were no crashes.

I always think that it was our angels looking out for us. After all, if it's not your time to pass on, then, whatever happens, you simply will not pass on.

My experience was a fairly subtle example of my dad and I being protected by angels. Some of the following stories are a lot more fascinating...

MARIE SERIO DELLAVALLE
Retired
New Haven, Connecticut, United States

It was a hot and humid summer day in 2005. I had just returned home from work and I was anxious to change into something cooler and relax before preparing supper.

Rarely did I sit and watch television immediately after arriving home from work, but the humidity was so intense that I decided to relax and cool off for a while. Tossing my lunch bag on the counter and slipping off my shoes, I hurried to change my clothes and plop onto the couch in the living room.

I switched on the living room ceiling fan. Soon, the large, thin blades were whizzing round and round on the highest speed and I quickly felt cooler.

I propped myself up at one end of the couch in my usual spot by the armrest, so I could sit a little higher to glance out of the double window on my right, watching for the mailman. After a few minutes, a firm but soft, audible voice said to me, "Go and get a glass of cold water, and then go and check your e-mail...*just for a few minutes.*" I found myself doing as I was told.

Many times throughout the years I have experienced this same voice, so I did not hesitate to follow its instructions. As if I was guided, I pulled myself off the couch to take the few steps to the kitchen. I poured some sparkling water in a tall glass and found the largest ice cubes I could to chill the water.

I pivoted left to head out of the kitchen and remembered the voice saying to me, "Go and check your e-mail...*just for a few minutes.*" I wasn't in the mood, but forced myself to go. I walked another 15 steps to the spare room where my computer was. The spare room was directly across from the living room, with a very narrow hallway and a dividing wall between them. My favorite program was on television, and as anxious as I was to go back on the couch and watch it under the cool breeze from the fan, I could not budge from the computer.

Suddenly, from the living room, I heard a pounding BANG! CRASH! BANG! I froze in my chair, frantic, thinking someone was breaking into my house through the double front windows. I became extremely nervous and began to shake.

A minute later, there was yet another pounding BANG! BANG! This time, I was able to escape the chair and cautiously, *ever so cautiously*, tiptoe across the hall to peek into my living room hoping to see what was going on. I was overtaken by fear—I did not know what to expect. Were there intruders?

The windows were intact. The couch was as I'd left it. There was no visible sign of anyone breaking in. So, was I crazy to hear all the banging and crashing? Maybe the heat and humidity had gotten to me. My eyes slowly panned the living room and it was then that I noticed the decorative dish that hung on the wall next to the front windows was no longer there.

I let my guard down and felt less nervous, but still curious. A strange spinning sound from above caused me to look up at the fan. I noticed it was spinning in a lopsided manner. I reached over to the switch on the wall, shutting the fan off to stop the annoying rumbling sound. The spinning slowed down, and when it came to a complete stop, I realized that two out of the five blades were missing. Where were they?

I gingerly walked over to the couch, my eyes still panning left to right, and then I scanned the rest of the room to search for the two missing blades. The couch was almost right up against the back wall—there was only about 10 inches of space between them. To the right was another single window, but it was untouched and no windows were broken.

Just then, I looked down on the side of the couch, and, inches from where I sat, I saw the dish on the floor in shattered pieces. My heart dropped. I slowly walked closer to the couch, then knelt on it, facing the wall so I could look behind it.

My heart was pounding and I gasped to see that both fan blades lay on top of each other on the floor. If I had been sitting on the couch, those fan blades would have smashed into my upper body and probably my head and neck too. They may even have killed me instantly.

There were no words to describe how upset I felt. The whole incident took *"just a few minutes."* The strange experience left many questions in my mind. First, was "something" out to get me? Could it have been a demonic spirit?

Also, it was very strange that *two* blades flew off the moving fan about a minute apart and came off at *exactly at the same place* where I would have been sitting. The other walls sported framed pictures, a bookcase, glassware, and even a television, yet nothing but that special dish was destroyed.

The heat and humidity were usually uncomfortable, but I could tolerate it and did not put the fan on in the living room very often. This particular fan was about five years old. I had never given any thought to such a freaky experience happening. I had never, in my whole life, heard of this kind of accident or knew of anyone who had a ceiling fan whose blades had dislodged and flown off.

Another shocking "coincidence" caused me to think that I was the target of this because the windows, to the right of me, as well as the one on the wall in back of the couch, were right there within a couple feet of where I sat and they were *not* broken. The strong banging and crashing had to be the blades hitting the dish and the wall directly behind the couch where I usually sat, but there were no holes, no slices, no cuts, and no damage to the wall at all.

I would have thought that the force from spinning so fast and being released from the ceiling unit would have bounced them off the wall and into other parts of the room, causing damage to so many other vulnerable things and landing in obvious places.

I had the fan taken down from the ceiling and I retrieved the two fan blades from behind the couch. They had no damage. I researched the company name brand and called them. They advised me that this product was sold only at a well-known home improvement center and that I would have to deal with them. In the meantime, I got in touch with a lawyer, but he never called back.

Aside from everything, I thank God and my guardian angels for watching over me, saving me from what could have been a horrible tragedy. Luckily, it wasn't the first time an audible voice had come to me. This time it saved my life and strengthened my faith in God, and my faith in the Light, all in *"just a couple of minutes."*

SUZANNE SLAW

Spiritual Coach and Energy Healer
Virginia Beach, Virginia, United States

It was March 2004. I was into the second year of living in the beautiful 19th-Century farmhouse I had bought after my husband (and high-school sweetheart) and I divorced. I had decided to move away from where I called home for many years to start over. I took my dream job in public education and everything fell into place perfectly. I went to great lengths to make my home a perfect space of positive energy, as this was the first home I had ever purchased on my own. I was in pure joy, even being seven miles away from any shops. The acreage and additional building that was originally a barn added to the sheer beauty and magic of the place. I called it my own little paradise. I felt I was finally home.

Throughout the pressures and stresses of my new position, working long hours and not taking enough time for myself, inevitably I became ill. I had often suffered from severe seasonal allergies that would often incapacitate me if I didn't head to the doctor's office for another round of antibiotics, or, on the rare occasion, a nebulizer treatment. So I brushed off this feeling as just another allergy attack because spring was approaching and my property was filled with flowers, trees, and blooms. A week passed and I treated myself with the usual holistic remedies I had learned to use before stepping into the pharmacy for a prescription.

By then, the dis-ease had set in so deeply that I was diagnosed with early pneumonia. No wonder I couldn't breathe or even exist in a normal frame of mind. I was relegated to bed rest for at least three days to allow an antibiotic to take effect. My mother had recently moved from her home two and a half hours away to be with a new companion, and fortunately she was now only 30 minutes away, but she worked full-time as a high-school nurse and couldn't come at any given moment to assist me. I was okay with that, as I have always been very independent. Nevertheless, being this ill for the first time in my adult life and finding myself completely alone was a new adventure for me.

During the first two days, I simply rested. My secretary at the time, who lived 30 miles away, brought me care packages of chicken soup and orange juice, leaving it on my back porch so as not to disturb my sleep. I always knew when she had left and would trek downstairs from my bedroom for some nourishment. By the end of the second day I began to feel a little better, but I wasn't in the clear yet.

To pass the time, I would call my maternal grandmother, who lives outside of Chicago, for encouragement and support. She would pray for me over and over as we spoke and after we had finished speaking. She is a devout Roman Catholic and has always invoked a powerful energy for the family. I was so grateful to chat with her, as both she and I lived alone and it kept us both company. I remember to this day how she very urgently warned me to be careful of the night sweats. With pneumonia, or its onset, one sweats profusely while in the sleep state as the physical body purges the toxic energy of the illness. Grandma was adamant that I wake up and change my pajamas so I wouldn't get chills from being in wet clothing. I told her I would be extra vigilant of this. I hung up the phone, made myself some soup, then retreated to bed for a good night's rest. I remember lying down, saying my prayers and blessings, then drifting into a very deep slumber.

At around 2:30 a.m., I bolted upright in my bed. It was a very mechanical motion, and was dazed and foggy from the intense sleep that I had been startled out of. I felt soaked in my pajamas and a thought came to me with Grandma's words: "Be careful of the night sweats." I sent her a prayer of thanks while still in my twilight state of mind.

My bed sat opposite a small portion of wall where my dresser was positioned. To the right of my dresser was a hearth, closed up since the days in the last century when homes had fireplaces in almost every room. There was still a mantel there, upon which I had created an altar with figurines of Angels, Archangels, Angel cards, and all of my sacred treasures.

As I sat in my upright position, completely dazed, a beautiful Light emerged before me. I thought about my state of mind and how dreamy I felt, but it was as though this energy was placing me in such a state. This Light was the most ethereal Light I have ever experienced in my entire life, and the Love that emanated from it was like receiving a hug, the kind where you feel as though your stuffing will pop out. I continued to focus on this Light; I was virtually in a dream state, yet very awake. It wasn't a very big beacon, more of an orb, perhaps two feet in diameter, hovering over my dresser. I lay back down while absorbing the energy of this beautiful and magnificent experience, continuing to watch it, connect with it, be it (throughout all this I was in drenched pajamas and not following my grandma's advice). That is when the size of the orb grew. It extended from about two feet off of the floor and to the 12-foot ceiling in sort of an oval shape, and then the top portion of the Light appeared to extend itself across the ceiling about two feet. I was amazed. Was I dreaming? What was this? It felt wonderful and I felt safe in its presence. Then the massive oval white Light energy began to form into a being. As I watched it take form, I felt such magnificent and protective power, that everything was okay and that I had nothing to fear. In an instant, as I lay there with my covers pulled up to my chin, the most beautiful Angel appeared.

It grew larger and its Light literally illuminated the whole room. Then the Angel became animated, its long hair flowing in a nonexistent breeze, its wings flapping just enough so it hovered before me. The robe the Angel wore moved with each motion of its wings. There was an Angel in my room watching over me! I lay there, my eyes not believing what was happening. I even rubbed my eyes to make sure I was indeed awake. I was filled with so much Love, such an overwhelming feeling of protection that I began to drift back to sleep. I slept deeply and awoke with a greater level of healing than I had felt upon retiring the night before.

When morning dawned, I awoke and sat up, still in a dreamy half-awake frame of mind. I rubbed my eyes, drank some water from the glass on my bedside table, and then realized something. I put the glass down and felt my chest, arms, back, and legs. *Good gracious! Where is my pajama top?* I wore to bed a button-down flannel shirt with matching pants—pink-dotted with little angel fairies holding wands. My pajama pants were still on, but not the top! I sat there for a moment trying to make sense of this, when suddenly I saw it. My usual habit if I need to remove my night-shirt is to take it off and throw it on the other side of the bed or on the floor. This morning it was different. My pajama top was at the foot of my bed, perfectly folded with the sleeves brought to-gether and the shirt folded in half, as if I had just done the laundry and prepared to put it away. Not only that, but the shirt, perfectly folded, was positioned as if someone at the foot of the bed had laid it there, to be put away in the closet. In other words, the collar of my shirt was facing me as I sat in bed, the crease of the shirt across its middle faced my dresser. Dumbstruck, I climbed out of bed and went to stand at the foot of my bed to get a better look. I put my hand on the shirt and leaned over to smell it. It was perfectly dry and smelled as though it had just come out of the dryer. I had been taken care of by an Angel! I spontaneously dropped to my knees and cried pure tears of joy, giving the most heartfelt thanks I could offer. I received a telepathic message after I finished my prayer of thanks and before I stood from my kneeling position. It said, "You are so welcome, Suzanne. I am here with you, for I am here to protect you and see that you are well. I am Michael. I am always with you."

The evening after, I called my grandma and told her what had happened. All she said was, "I told you, you need to be careful of those night sweats! I felt worried about you, so I sent you a little help since I couldn't be there. I'm glad He pulled you through."

SHARON MAY SAUBOORAH
Psychic
Enfield, United Kingdom

Angel Protection

In the early days of our relationship and before marriage, I lived in Luton and my husband lived in London. This meant that on numerous occasions my husband and I traveled to and fro on the motorway.

One night we were traveling home in the early hours, and, as usual, he was driving. It was around 5 a.m. and there was hardly anyone around. My husband had opened the window, as he was feeling tired. I suggested that perhaps we should pull over and rest a little, but he insisted that he would be okay and that I needn't worry. So I settled into the passenger seat, although I still felt slightly worried.

It's funny, but I have always had the knack of sensing when something might happen—you know, that feeling you get in the pit of your stomach, almost like a warning. This was one of those times and although I felt exhausted, I kept looking at my husband, noticing how his eyes were almost closing. However, the more I asked him if he was okay, the more cross he became. So to avoid an argument, I stopped asking him.

My husband drove down the slip road that led onto the empty motorway. It was quite surreal not seeing any other vehicles, except for the occasional truck hurtling along. I felt exhausted and my eyes started to close when I suddenly felt someone shake my arm to awaken me. I looked up at my husband, whose eyes were closed. Suddenly the car veered over to the right and somehow the two wheels on the driver's side mounted the central reservation barrier. I screamed, which startled my husband and he opened his eyes. There was nothing he could do to get our car back onto the road, as he had no control over it.

Suddenly, we both felt the car being lifted up on my husband's side. The car was lifted off of the barrier, and then the next minute all four wheels were back on the road. My husband drove over to the hard shoulder and stopped the car. He looked at me and asked, "What happened? How the hell did the car get off the barrier?"

We both got out and walked around to check the tires on the driver's side, and there on the wheel was a single white feather. We both looked at each other in complete shock. I smiled and remembered how my arm was shaken to awaken me.

That night, I honestly believe that an Angel or my Father's spirit came and lifted the car back onto the road. I believe that my husband and I were protected and helped by an Angel or Spirit. The white feather was a sign that we were being looked after.

Chapter 8:
Premonitions

About 10 years ago, six months before my sister gave birth to her first baby, I predicted that she would be born on November 6th. The date popped into my mind one day, out of nowhere, as I was taking a shower. I had no idea where the date had come from but decided to trust it. I started telling everyone around me that my sister's baby daughter would be born on November 6th, which was also the birth date of my elderly Nan, who was in her early 90s. I had moved to Spain by this point and still lived with my parents. At around 3'oclock in the morning on November 6th the phone rang. I heard my dad get up wearily to answer it. I could not hear the conversation but in my heart knew that my sister or her husband was calling to say that she had given birth. The next morning, my parents confirmed that she had indeed given birth to her first daughter: Charli Knight.

After living with my parents in Spain for nine months, I finally moved into my own new-build apartment. A few years after living there, I bought a new car. It was black, and I had the logo of the magazine I owned and ran stuck onto the car for brand recognition and so that potential advertisers would see my phone number and hopefully call to place their adverts! It was a hot day in summer, and, as the tourists had started to arrive, parking outside my apartment proved difficult. There were no spaces, so I drove up a little hill to a secret place: a plot of land where cars sometimes parked during the busier summer months. As I parked, a feeling crossed my mind that perhaps I shouldn't park there, as on this particular day mine was the only car. I shrugged the thought off and went into my apartment to start working on my computer. In the midst of sending e-mails to clients, another thought came to me that my phone was about to start ringing, and in my mind's eye I was shown an image of my car. I answered my phone to a Spanish man who said he had gotten my number off the side of my car. He said he owned the land where my car was parked and he was leveling it all off with machinery. He asked that I come and move my car.

More recently, I saw a photo of my husband-to-be on Facebook and instantly knew that we were meant to be together, even though he had a partner at the time, and I had no idea how that would happen. A strong feeling arrived in my heart, and it was a sense of *knowing*. I didn't doubt for a second that we would end up together. Two and a half years later we met, and pretty quickly started a long-distance relationship between Spain and the United States, seeing each other every three or four months when we could. Two years after that we married and we now live together in the United States. I also knew that I would end up living in the States, as did various friends with psychic abilities, but that's a different story...

Maybe by reading the following stories, you'll remember incidents of your own when you were able to successfully predict events before they happened...

ANGELA DENT
Retired Restaurant Owner
La Viñuela, Spain

My Mother Calling Me

I was very close to my father. He was a dear man, loved by everyone. He always came to me for advice, and in the same way, I went to him for advice. When he was diagnosed with lung cancer at the age of 67, it was a great shock. My mother was devastated and wanted to be with him all the time. Even though we said he would be at home for his final moments and never enter a hospital, it was decided by the medics that he should go into a hospice for a few days to give us a rest.

I had a very demanding business at the time and three children but I took care of Mum and Dad's needs every day. Dad went into the hospice but Mum decided she couldn't leave him so she stayed there and I visited daily.

One morning while I was asleep I heard my mother calling me for help. I saw her lying on the ground with a white van about to run her over. I awoke my husband and told him about my dream, and I also noted the time as I had a strange feeling that something had happened. It was 8:30 a.m. When I got to the hospice my mother was not around, and when I asked where she was no one would tell me. All of a sudden she appeared, flung her arms around me, and started to cry. I asked her what had happened and she told me that she was very lucky to be here. She had popped out for a walk and as she was stepping off the pavement she fell and a parked van started to reverse onto her legs. The driver of the van had not seen her. Luckily, the receptionist saw from her window and shouted to the driver to stop. Mother was taken to the nearest hospital to make sure she was okay. Apart from some bruising she was fine. I asked the staff why I hadn't been notified and they said Mum had told them not to worry me. I asked what time this had happened, and I wasn't at all surprised to hear that it was 8:30 a.m. I later asked Mum if she remembered the color of the van, and she said, "It was white."

A few days after we had laid Dad to rest, I was awoken during the night by someone brushing my cheek. I looked up and saw Dad smiling at me. I asked him what he was doing there, as he was no longer with us, and he replied, "I just wanted to make sure that you're okay." I went back to sleep with a lovely warm feeling.

On the morning of the day my son, Simon, died, he came home from being out the night before and smoked a cigarette on the porch. This was unusual for him as normally he would go straight to bed after coming home in the early hours. On any other night I would have told him off for staying out all night, but on this particular day I felt a weird sensation and something told me not to say anything. Instead I asked if he was okay, and he replied by asking me if I was okay. I got the strangest feeling that I was never going to see him again and that he was going to die. I felt so sure that I went and told Ken, my husband, that I was sure we were going to lose Simon. He replied, "Whatever has made you think that?" I couldn't explain it, but I just knew. When the dreadful call came in the night to tell us that Simon had been in a car accident, I said to Ken, "That's it; Simon has gone." He told me not to be silly. I asked the person on the phone if he had died and she told me, "No, but he is in a very bad way." At this point, he was in fact already dead. I phoned my brother and told him about the accident and that Simon had died, as I was so sure.

For eight months prior to Simon's death, I had been suffering with a pain in the right side of my neck. On this particular night, after hearing the news that Simon had passed away, my pain became so unbearable that I wept and told Ken that the next day I would go to a medic. As I said those words, all of a sudden the candle, which was lit by a photo of Simon, started to strobe. I asked Simon to take away my pain, and instantly the pain went and it hasn't returned since. Ken is a non-believer but even he had to admit that there was no other explanation.

ALISON HENDERSON
Journalist
Winchester, United Kingdom

My first husband was a clairvoyant-medium and misused his many psychic gifts, leaving a lot of people damaged, including myself. Not long after my husband left me I was in a fragile state emotionally. It took me a considerable time to finally heal with the help of my wonderful family and incredible friends.

One day there was a New Age gathering taking place in the neighboring county, so some friends and I drove to the event. I have occasional premonitions, and on the drive I said to my friends, "I'm going to meet someone at this event whom I know." I felt terrified, as my first reaction was that my now-estranged husband would be there, either giving clairvoyance or one of his spiritual lectures. However, I did not ask to stop the car or turn around.

When we arrived at the venue, a small village hall, we were ushered into the kitchen to get a cup of coffee before the day's events began. A striking-looking couple were in the kitchen and we were introduced to them: Christine and Florian.

To my utter amazement, I realized that I knew him. We had never met before, but his picture had been stuck up on my wall when I was 12! He was the drummer with a British band called Curved Air, the first group whose music I really got into. He was particularly memorable because of his good looks, along with his exotic name.

So I came right out and said to him, "I know who you are! You're the drummer with Curved Air." As it had been the greater part of 20 years since they became very well known in the UK, he was quite taken aback that I remembered who he was, and we spent the remainder of the day speaking about their music and life in general.

This meeting happened in the early 1990s, and our paths have crossed a couple of times since, as Curved Air are still touring together with their wonderful singer Sonja Kristina, my lifelong heroine. It was such a joy to finally meet her. And all because of a premonition.

Chapter 9:
Healing

My own healing story can be found in full at the beginning of *The Light: A Book of Wisdom*. But for the benefit of those who have not read that book, I'll share a portion of the story here.

In the midst of my debilitating depression, when I desperately wanted to know my life purpose in this lifetime, but felt I didn't have one, I was guided to attend a Mind-Body-Spirit festival via a series of synchronistic events. At the festival, right before I planned to leave, I spotted a stand called Mind Body Soul Healing and felt drawn to go and take a look. As I was reading a leaflet on the stand, a man's smiling face popped up from the other side. He introduced himself as Richard Waterborn, and our brief conversation led me to try some cellular healing sessions with him, which is healing on an energetic level from deep within our body's cells.

At the time, I'd just been diagnosed with an overactive thyroid gland, and the doctor told me that I would have to take medication for the rest of my life to keep it under control. I understood how energetic and emotional imbalances can cause illness and dis-ease, so I was determined to get to the bottom of my condition and heal it from the inside out, without needing to take the chemicals present in most medicines. Back then, little did I know what a huge impact this series of healing sessions would have on my life. During the first session, I burst into tears and old emotions resurfaced, ready to be healed. An unpleasant experience that had occurred when I was 17 also came up, and as I lay down on the healing bed and did a deep breathing exercise, my entire body convulsed for more than an hour, as I let go of all the trapped energy and emotion surrounding that experience.

Right after the first session, I began to have spiritual experiences on a regular basis. It felt as though my third eye had opened, and messages and sights from the other side were pouring through to wake me up to what really lay in neighboring realms. In the weeks and months that followed, my life completely transformed. After one of the healing sessions, Richard told me that my body had turned into liquid—the cells were literally transforming and reforming in front of his eyes—and at this point he knew that deep healing had occurred. And it had. Magic started to happen right after that, and now I can say, with my hand on my heart, that I am no longer the same person I was back then.

And, when I went for a follow-up blood test at the doctor's, my practitioner was absolutely shocked. "Your thyroid level is completely back to normal," she said. "There's no need for you to take any medication."

Our body is so powerful that it is quite possible to heal even serious illnesses in an instant—especially with teamwork from our soul. All we need to do is believe, have faith, and know.

So, if you currently have a condition and you seek healing, perhaps the stories in this chapter will inspire you about what is possible. And it doesn't necessarily have to be a physical illness—Hannah Davis's story, for example, reveals the emotional healing from which many of us would benefit, in order to transform our life in magical ways.

ROISHEEN KEATING
Retired Childminder
Torre del Mar, Spain

One evening I attended a shamanic ritual with someone who didn't want to go alone. I had no idea what might happen at this ritual, as I didn't know anything about it. During the early hours of the morning, while it was still dark, a Peruvian Shaman traced sticks around our bodies, and when he found something out of alignment he hit that part with the sticks—not directly onto our bodies, but onto the sticks that he held in place there.

I had suffered with a painful hip for a number of years due to lifting children while child-minding. During my turn he hit the stick on my left hip very hard with his other stick, and a huge spark of white Light flew from my body. I didn't understand why at the time, but when I got home I realized that my hip didn't hurt anymore. That was more than two years ago and it hasn't hurt since.

SARA EIKEN-BENTLEY
Freedom Fighter
London, United Kingdom

Two years ago, before I was due to go to hospital to remove two bilateral ovarian cysts, I spent a few weeks embracing all of the beautiful books beside my bed, including *Life Lessons* by Elizabeth Kübler-Ross, and my Law of Attraction books. I had gone deeply into the "what ifs" and I was feeling scared and concerned about the future. I was worried about losing my ovaries. My grandmother had had major surgery on her ovaries, and it resulted in a total hysterectomy. Growing up I'd witnessed all of the turmoil and trauma that had surrounded this operation. Quietly, I was somewhat terrified!

What happened next was truly amazing! I closed my eyes, placed my hands on either side of my ovaries, and gently felt a tingling under my fingers. Then I surrendered and asked for help.

Moments later, a bright, luminous, piercing-light being, tall and female, hovered to the right side of me above my bed. Her arms were outstretched and waving over my stomach area. Within seconds my abdomen area seemed to open up, and out flew hundreds of tiny, bright, blue and white butterflies! Afterward, I felt calm, truly at peace, and I knew that everything would be okay. And it was! My operation went beautifully, I healed, and the cysts were both found to be benign.

I am now having another opportunity to heal on an even deeper level as I embrace other hormonal changes that are starting to take place in my body.

Tricia Gabbitas
Poet and Songwriter/Retired Secretary
North Yorkshire, United Kingdom

In my 40s I had a problem with my right shoulder. I had a "spur"—an overgrowth of bone that prevented me from raising my arm. I could hardly move my arm from front to back either.

One day a friend invited me to join her at her church—Huddersfield Christian Fellowship. I hadn't been there before. It was a "happy clappy" type of church, and very soon everyone was clapping, singing, and raising their arms to God. Suddenly both my arms went up above my head, without me even trying! I was amazed and burst into tears. It was claimed as a holy healing.

A few weeks later I was asked to give my testimony to the church. I had worked out what I was going to say, but then, just before I left home for church, I read "The Word for Today" from United Christian Broadcasters. The first words it said for that Sunday were, "Child of God, before you give your testimony, don't forget people who have not had answers to their prayers." I was absolutely amazed! I changed what I was going to say and reached many more people with God's message. It is wonderful how Jesus leads us, if we will let Him.

Hannah M. Davis
Author and Writing Mentor
Stamford, United Kingdom

Love and Light

"Love and light" binds together two of the most potent words in the English language like a pair of old lovers. How many times do you see it in a spiritual greeting, at the end of an e-mail or card, in a blessing, or in a goodbye?

It is interesting to note that the word *photosynthesis*, the process by which plants transform light energy into chemical energy in order to survive, also has its roots in light and love. *Photo* means "light" and *thesis* means "coming together." So you could say light brings two things together, and in the case of a plant, the result of this generally means it will open up and flower.

It is the same for humans. Just as a bud seeks sunlight, how many people across the world seek a soul's mate in order to blossom with the joy of true love? Unfortunately, for many people, the love that comes with meeting your soul's mate remains tantalizingly out of reach. But why is this? And how can light be the answer?

My Story

I share my own story because, like most people at one point in their lives, I chased love. My story started in England with damp, grey clouds and a broken heart, which is why in my mid-20s I moved south to Andalucia, Spain, to an area where there were more than 320 days of sunshine each year and a huge multicultural population—and where I was sure to find the man of my dreams.

I lived in a beautiful white-washed village in the mountains, where the light bounced off the houses and orange trees grew by the side of the road and the smell of their blossoms filled the air. For more than 10 years I soaked in the sunlight, lived a creatively fulfilled life, and felt happy.

But there was one thing missing, and that thing was love.

Guys said I was smart, attractive, and witty. I had achieved a number of things I was very proud of—I had traveled the world, run a marathon, and written a book that had received great reviews. Professionally I felt at the top of my game. But none of that seemed to matter, because at the age of 37 I was still single.

The Wrong Kind of Love

I'd always fallen in love with the wrong type of man, and, even after leaving England, I still ended up with a bruised heart more times than I care to mention. In fact, I'd been rejected so many times I'd begun to think there was something wrong with me.

Even when I did end up in relationships, why did they feel so dark and heavy? Why did I cry more than I laughed? Where was the light and joy that other couples seemed to have?

After yet another failed relationship my heart could take no more, and I came to a point in my life where I realized things needed to change. I simply could not bear the thought of putting myself (and all my friends and family) through another doomed love affair. I even contemplated moving countries in order to start again, but here is when the epiphany struck: no matter how sunny my life on the outside, no matter where I lived, no matter who I met, I needed the sun to shine on the inside too.

In other words, in order to meet my soul's mate, I had to take responsibility for what I had been co-creating in my relationships.

Search for the Light

On a recommendation from a good friend, Keidi, the author of this book, I went to see a wonderful intuitive healer on the coast. I left everything and everyone I knew to go and live by the sea so I could benefit from his sessions and go through the healing process.

The sessions involved me lying flat on my back and taking one deep breath after another. This was all there was to it. But that first session was the most profound moment of my life. I reached into myself, deeper than I had ever cared to look before, shone a light into my soul, and saw a little girl cowering in the shadows who was petrified of love.

I saw a woman who didn't even believe she deserved to be loved—who had picked unequal relationships because that was all she thought she was worth. I was far too scared of anything as transformational, as wonderful, as honest, as deserving as true love.

I was at crunch time. Did I want to change? To bud? To open up? Or did I want to stay coiled up in the darkness, protecting myself but forever missing out on the deep spiritual awakening that true love can bring?

In short, was I ready to open up to the light?

It sounds like an easy decision, but in fact, in order for anyone to truly change they must first go deeply within, and this is often the scariest, hardest journey of all. It's far more straightforward to get on an airplane than it is to journey inside the body. What lies hidden in the darkest recesses? What beliefs must be laid bare for you to finally acknowledge them? What stuck energy must you somehow let go of?

But was any of this worse than staying exactly how I was?

Opening Up to Love and Light

There comes a point in anyone's life when the decision to remain tight in a bud is far more painful than the decision to open up to the light and blossom. I was ready to open up, so I took part in more healing sessions, and although they were often turbulent and emotional, I slowly started to address my beliefs about my self-worth and allowed the fears to drop away.

After the course of nine months—the time it takes to create new life—I had breathed in enough light to undergo my own photosynthesis and transform my deepest fears into something far more beautiful and bright.

I learned how to open up to love.

Now I just needed to find him!

I publicly set the intention on Facebook that I would meet my soul mate at the beginning of 2012. I believe that intentions have more kick when made in front of other people, and my comment received a huge amount of interest from people all over the world.

It was as if I had planted a seed and all these other people were nourishing it with their support. My next step was to do everything I could to shower this seed with even more light and positive intent.

I moved house again, this time inland to a beautiful villa tucked away in the Spanish countryside. Scented jasmine flowered in the patio. Bougainvillea climbed romantically over the porch. The Med shimmered on the horizon, and at sunset the mountains of Morocco appeared as exotic and magical beacons from a different world.

It was the perfect love nest!

Less than one week after taking the lease and only six weeks after putting my intention on Facebook, I met Chris.

I knew straight away he was the man I had been waiting for all my life.

Later that evening, we took a walk around the village and ended up standing under an orange tree to watch the sun go down.

Time to Blossom

I didn't know this at the time, but orange trees are actually a symbol of love. And if you've ever smelt orange blossom wafting through the breeze on a warm spring day, then you'll know why. It really does smell of romance.

The orange tree became our symbol, which is apt because orange trees only grow in abundant sunshine. One year from the day we met Chris dropped to one knee and asked me to be his wife, and after I had sobbed on his shoulder in front of the entire restaurant I said yes!

Five months later, we got married in a beautiful ceremony in an old country estate in England, in a stunning room called The Orangery. It was a warm summer's day and the sunlight streamed in through the glass windows, filling the room with the most beautiful natural light. The ceremony itself was full of laughter and our eyes twinkled with joy.

As I sit and write this, I gaze at our own orange tree, a wedding gift from a friend, which sits in our kitchen window, basking in the light. It has just started to bud, and hopefully this summer it will blossom and fill our house with the heady scent of romance.

To this date, I believe that if I had never gone through that deep spiritual journey of self-love, then I would never have met Chris. If I had never breathed in enough light, I would never have undergone my own photosynthesis, and I would never know what real, true love could be like.

And that's why love and light always go hand in hand.

Because when you're brave enough to shine a light right down to the depths of your core then you will clearly see the parts of you that you *think* are unlovable, that have been holding you back from getting your heart's desire.

When you're courageous enough to start the change from the inside, then you will soon see the changes on the outside.

So send yourself love and light so you can bud and flower, opening up to all life's treasures, and then surely, if you haven't already done so, one day soon you will meet your own soul's mate.

Chapter 10:
Past Lives

One night I attended a shamanic healing ceremony facilitated by a Peruvian Shaman. Everyone took turns seeing the Shaman throughout the evening, and it went on until the early hours of the morning. He hit the sides of our bodies with sticks—not directly striking our bodies, but striking other sticks that he held in place. As the sticks collided, sparks would fly off— the more issues a person had, the brighter and more powerful the sparks.

He told me that I had a huge emotional issue in my chest and even after banging the area with his sticks and watching a mighty spark fly into the black night sky, he indicated that further healing work may still need to be done in the future.

I drove back to my apartment at 3 a.m., feeling exhausted. As soon as my head touched the pillow I exhaled a sigh of relief, but I didn't fall asleep right away. Instead, in my ultra-relaxed state, images flashed across my mind, one after the other. All of these images were of people...a soldier with a gun, an African man, a woman scrubbing doorsteps from the Victorian ages, a young Indian girl... And as each image appeared, the feelings of that person came with it. For example, when the solider turned up, I felt extreme guilt and sorrow; when the African man appeared I felt shame and a sense of worthlessness. Then it dawned on me—these were my past lives, coming up to be healed. It's no coincidence that this happened just hours after a shamanic healing session.

Another past-life related experience of the Light took place when I went to a psychic workshop hosted by a lady called Molly Ann Fairley. There were only seven other attendees, and at one point during the course of the two-day workshop, Molly asked us to sit in a circle, and she began asking each of us, one by one, to come to the middle, where she worked on us energetically. Immediately, I went into panic mode. One of my greatest fears was standing in front of a group of people. I had always worried about what people thought about me, and how I came across to others. Now, this fear seemed to have heightened incredibly, as standing in front of only seven people would not usually bother me. As I sat awaiting my turn, I began to tremble and my heartbeat quickened.

When my turn came, Molly called me into the circle. I froze and said I didn't want to. She looked at me, baffled, and said this was a great opportunity for me and that I'd be silly to miss it. I burst into tears on the spot and then ran outside into the fresh air. Moments later, another student ran outside to comfort me, and I spilled my heart to her, telling her how I had always felt afraid of standing in front of a group of people. After an hour or so of intense crying and body trembling, I got the courage to go back inside. With help from Molly and the support and unconditional love of the rest of the group, I took a deep breath and walked into the center of the circle. I closed my eyes and Molly released lifetime after lifetime of judgment by others, including one lifetime when I was hanged in front of a large audience for a crime I had not committed, and another lifetime when I had acid thrown in my face, again witnessed by a large group of people. It was no wonder I had always feared standing in front of people!

About six months after that healing, I received an e-mail inviting me to speak at a local venue about book writing and publishing, an area I had recently ventured into. My response startled me. In the past I would not have thought twice about firing back an e-mail with a "no," coupled with a lengthy explanation. But this time I truly felt that I could stand in front of 50 people without being a nervous wreck. Unfortunately, the timing and dates didn't work out, but a year later, I was invited to speak to an audience of 180 people on behalf of a charity called Infinite Love, in McAllen, Texas. There, I did a two-hour workshop in front of a room full of people, helping them to reawaken their Divine spark. This has now turned into my spiritual awakening workshop called The Light Experience. I spoke to lots of people, signed dozens of books, and even took home an envelope full of cash, made up of generous donations to *The Light*'s charity campaign.

Before I began the speaking event, a psychic lady asked to speak to me, so the organizers brought her into an adjacent room. She told me that she could see a past life where I'd been killed in front of an audience, and that back then I'd been forced to speak untruths by my leader. She said that in this lifetime I would get to speak my Truth instead, and that is what the Universe has planned for me.

Her words confirmed everything that Molly had told me, and when I walked on stage, after the first minute or so I felt strangely confident, and there were no signs of nerves at all.

MELANIE SIEVERNICH
Author
Marbella, Spain

Remember Who You Are

Growing up, my world was divided into two halves. I loved my life, and yet did not fully comprehend it. Deep within, there was a longing for something I could not explain. There was nothing to complain about in my childhood; it was rich in every way. I could not have chosen sweeter or more caring parents, but that did not stop me from searching the house for adoption papers to uncover my true origin—without success. My parents were my biological parents, so how come I ever doubted that? I am the spitting image of my father, and I had a photograph of my mother with a huge belly, ready to be taken to hospital to give birth to me. What I hadn't known then is that what I had been searching for was not to be found in my current life. I had to travel much further back in time.

Subconscious Memories

When I was in kindergarten and primary school, as soon as a girl with Eastern or Latin features joined my class, she immediately had my full attention. Mesmerized by the shiny black hair, almond eyes, and exotic features, I found there was something mysterious about them. That my attraction was triggered by my own heritage in several past lives was the greatest mystery of them all, and was only discovered many years later.

As I grew older, I felt a desperate urge to adopt a little girl from Nepal. I was a foreigner to the country, or so I thought, and couldn't wait to get to know it and its people. For a long time I neatly kept all the necessary adoption papers in a special file, because I had to be patient to fulfill my grandest dream: one had to be 35 years of age to adopt from Nepal as a single mother. Friends would often question my plans, fearing that I wouldn't feel the same love for an adopted child as I would for a biological child. But I knew this wasn't the case, and that the child's soul would be one and the same as a biological child of mine; only its eternal features would not match mine—at least not those of my current existence.

The Transformation

When I was old enough to start the three-year adoption process, my life was transformed, and, with it, my desire to adopt stopped. At 33 years old, I skeptically entered a yoga studio for the first time, which was the beginning of my journey within. The powerful yoga poses and exercises burst my blockages open and various past lives shot into my awareness. In my many visions, I discovered the roots of my habits, my interests, my suffering, and my grandest desires. It felt as if someone had handed me the key to the dungeon of my soul, which contained all the answers to my past, freeing me from heavy chains.

The little black-haired girl whom I had been so desperate to make friends with during childhood existed in one of my past lives, somewhere in Siam or Burma. In that lifetime I lived there with my parents, who worked hard under the blasting sun in a rice field. One day, my father picked me up into his arms and we left without any preparations. A long journey lay ahead of us, taking us to a new and unknown country. We were destitute, but a better future had been promised to my family. While witnessing myself as this little Asian girl of about 3 years old, I saw the reflection of my imaginary adoptive daughter from Nepal. We had the same shiny, fine black hair, chin length, with a fringe. Only our wardrobe differed. In my vision, I wore smudgy linen pants and a top in dismal shades.

Besides my many visions, I was regularly visited by Spirit. One Spirit I made friends with was a young monk from Kathmandu. On several nights, he sat at my side praying, while his loving and calm aura offered me a protective coat. His soft voice soothed me. Although I didn't understand his foreign, ancient language consciously, my subconscious appreciated and absorbed every single word. I wandered with him through the crowded, narrow streets of Nepal's capital, exploring a local suburb. He often slowly walked around the city's stupa, whose colorful and familiar top explained the fantasy figures I used to draw as a child, and my bias for vibrant colors.

Another spirit, of an elegant, elderly lady, has been with me for my entire lifetime. I had never been sure if she was real or no more than an illusion, until one night when she revealed her identity. She carried an amazing amount of pain, due to a lot of rejection and loss in her past lifetime during the 19th and 20th Centuries. She experienced her biggest rejection when her father had left her in an orphanage after the sudden death of her mother. I felt my spirit's pain within my own cells, and tears ran uncontrollably down my face.

Completing the Puzzle

Suddenly, I understood. The roots of my one great desire to adopt a little girl from Nepal were anchored in my past lives. And those lives weren't history; they were still fully present and a part of my being.

The answer to my desire was:

I am this little black-haired girl.

I am the orphan.

I am from Kathmandu.

By adopting this little girl from Nepal, I would bring part of my*self* home and unconsciously create a reunion with my own past.

Once I understood where my desire to adopt a little girl from Nepal came from, the desire fell away, like a scab that falls off of a healed wound, all by itself. My desire vanished in an instant, without me even noticing. I also no longer had the urge to visit Nepal. I already knew it by heart, now that I remembered my past.

We carry everything within. All desires, habits, interests, and suffering are anchored in our past lives. We drag it all along from one existence to the next, until we allow it to rise to the surface, and we finally remember who we are. That is when we let go.

SAMANTHA DONBAVAND
Regression Therapist and Hypnotherapist
San Pedro, Spain

Healing in the Light

Growing up, I saw Spirit, but back then I was too scared to so much as utter that word, so, like most natural healers, I kept quiet. When I trained as a holistic health practitioner and learned aromatherapy reflexology and counseling, I quickly realized how much I loved evoking change and helping others. And as my business blossomed so did the spiritual gifts I had within.

When my clients visited me for beauty and holistic therapy I intuitively felt energetic imbalances within their body and chakras, and I would start healing those areas.

Then an event occurred that changed my life forever... I was assaulted by a man who was obsessed with me.

As this happened, I could feel the pull and see my body, but I hovered above it. I didn't feel at all scared. Instead I felt a great peace, and the Light. I wanted to let go and be free, to venture deeper in the Light that surrounded me. I could still see my body below, and as I drifted in this space I thought of my beloved girls, aged 4 and 5, and knew that I couldn't give up and die. I returned to my body with a jolt, now feeling empowered to fight for my life and run. I repeated the names of my girls over and over in my head as I tried to get away. I made it home, but he was behind me. Twenty-four hours later, I realized that, though heavily injured, I was still alive. My near-death experience made me realize how precious life was. I felt very lucky and humbled to be alive.

A year later I was diagnosed with a chronic pain disorder for which I was told there was no cure. I had CRPS TYPE II with nerve damage in both hands. As a holistic health practitioner with a thriving practice, I didn't take this news well. I was told to give up my business, and I felt totally devastated. The next three months were a blur of pain, confusion, medication, and coping as best I could. At times I felt like giving up, and I'm so thankful for my daughters, who were my lights in the dark.

The specialist team and my consultant were both fantastic, but we all quickly realized that I was highly allergic to morphine. In fact, every medication I tried made me feel very ill both in my body and in my mind. As the months rolled on, my condition worsened. I was completely reliant on my two daughters and had to use a wheelchair and a stair-lift. Even holding a knife and fork was a struggle, and walking just a few steps was agony, as every part of my body throbbed with indescribable pain.

I decided to battle this disease using all of my holistic tools within. I thoroughly researched the horrific condition. I meditated, changed my diet, and tried everything to reduce the pain. I knew I had to get better for my girls, and I refused to believe that this would be with me for the rest of my life. Hypnotherapy reduced my pain a little and gave me a ray of hope. That "aha" moment came when I realized I could train in hypnotherapy and still be a therapist and help others. I researched for the best training in the field, and I was guided to RegressionAcademy.com. The more I read the more I smiled. I read about the positive results regression therapy had for chronic pain, and I knew this was what I wanted to do.

The regression training was like coming home. I found myself among others who had all had similar spiritual experiences—highly intelligent people from all walks of life with gifts to share. I was no longer afraid to talk about my spiritual experiences, my ability to channel spirit, and how I saw energetic imbalances within people. My heart embraced this new direction in my life and I couldn't wait to be trained in the specialist field.

My first regression therapy session blew me away. I remembered working in an orphanage in the 1600s, and I recalled my deep love for all of these children. A fire broke out and I couldn't save them all. My arms were burned and I decided to die with a child named Jacob. The energetic imprint/soul memory of guilt and pain had been stored within my arms. I asked for forgiveness and felt the vibrational energetic healing through my body. It made a whirring sound, and it felt like I had been given new arms. The relief was immediate. I moved my arms and legs. I felt lighter, and my pain had reduced enormously. I couldn't believe it. Throughout that year as I trained, further past-life regressions and spiritual regressions enabled me to be the person who I am now, and I feel deeply blessed that I believed and listened to my heart.

This experience enabled me to understand and make sense of who I am, to not feel shame for speaking the truth of my work, and to continue to educate people, because, for some, the word *spiritual* is still shrouded with fear.

When I qualified in regression therapy six years ago I knew I should live in a warmer climate and intuitively felt a need to bring a spark of awareness and hope to Spain. I have now been in remission from CRPS for five years. Moving to a warmer climate has helped my health enormously, and my spiritual growth has been tremendous.

I find it empowering that regression therapy is being recognized and used in hospitals. It changed my life. It has also helped hundreds of my clients unlock and unblock their answers within, helping them improve emotionally, mentally, and spiritually.

DEBBIE EDWARDS
Medium and Author
Bonners Ferry, Idaho, United States

I'd like to share an unusual yet romantic love story with you about how I met my husband, Matthew. The year we first met is a little sketchy in my memory. After all, several hundred years have passed since then. But if I were to connect to a particular time period, it would be the early 1600s, when we were alive and well in Europe.

My father was the king of a moderately wealthy kingdom and prided himself on the assets and notoriety he had accrued in his lineage of rule. He was an eccentric king and had his passions—mainly women and song—and he had become quite the skilled pianist in his youth, which stayed with him throughout adulthood. He enjoyed his wealth, but for the most part, he didn't strive to conquer or take anyone else's wealth unless his soldiers and knights were met in battle by an opposing force he could not reconcile with. He insisted on being loved by the people of his kingdom and his reputation became his bible, which he preached from. His speeches became like sermons and he obsessed over maintaining his power and control over others.

As he aged, he grew distracted by his obsessions and failed to realize that his strength, or the loyalty given to him by the people, was slipping away. They grew hungry for change and resented the excess he paraded in front of them. They became intolerant and defiant, and word of this spread to neighboring lands. This rumor revealed to a young, arrogant prince that soon he would take the throne of his father and have an opportunity to rule both his own kingdom and the kingdom of my father.

At this time, all our sense of security waivered. I was young and soon to be married to the man who is now my husband in this life. I was in love with my father's most loyal soldier and knight, and he was in love with me. He had won my affection from the moment we met, and when we could, we would sneak past the orchards and spend time under the large oak tree that guarded the edge of the fields beyond the castle gates. This is where we would hold each other and where he would make me laugh. This is where I would fall asleep in his arms and tell him stories about adventures I had heard of that took place in distant lands and countries far away, places that were only said to exist by the word of gypsies. My father had made sure I knew of the world and that I was well educated so that I could raise intelligent sons. My father had grand plans for me, and the life he expected me to live, including his own plans of who I should marry and why. As much as he adored Matthew and respected him, Matthew was not a prince, or a king, and my father wanted as much for me as he could arrange. I spent my youth living up to that expectation without the opportunity to harness my own dreams. Overall, I was mostly content and dreamed of the time when my love and I could marry, and my father would see that I had made the right choice.

When news broke that the young arrogant prince had overthrown his own father and taken hostage of his kingdom, my father learned that we were soon to be invaded by a large army of knights and soldiers that had been fiercely trained for victorious battles. My father knew that his own laziness and arrogance in his power had made his kingdom weaker than his rival. He simply wasn't prepared. The news of battle surprised him and he sat alone with the decision he had to make: go to war or surrender.

Matthew, being loyal to the king and confident of victory, stood beside the king with other trusted knights and soldiers who were willing to give their life to defend the kingdom, and who rallied for permission to go to battle. He knew that even though they were outnumbered, they could achieve victory so long as they followed the plans he devised. But my father wasn't roused by their intentions or confidence. He sat in his chair and mulled over what he was going to do, toying with the notion that, instead, he could flee and abandon the castle. He considered taking what assets he could and traveling to another region where he could rebuild what he had built once before and rule a new land with little opposition. It would be a way to escape without the need for battle *or* surrender. That way, he could retain his dignity and reputation.

Matthew was confused and furious, along with several other soldiers and knights. It was a hasty decision, and if my father abandoned his kingdom, the people would surely suffer. Nevertheless, Matthew left the king's chambers and waited for answers. At that time he grouped together with the other men and met around a campfire. He spoke from his heart and suggested battle plans that he knew would work. He drew maps in the sand and showed the other men. He knew that if he could just gain the confidence of the king in his plans, it would be successful. But what he didn't expect was that one of the soldiers in his camp had become a traitor. This soldier, who was training to become a knight, had betrayed them all and had aligned with the neighboring kingdom for favors of his own wealth, power, and importance in exchange for arranging a favor in return for the new young king. He had been one of Matthew's closest friends. They had trained together and laughed together. They were like brothers, and he was the last person Matthew would have suspected to have betrayed anyone, especially him.

Matthew walked into the king's chamber the following morning to consult with him about battle plans, only to discover he wasn't the first to arrive. The other soldier, his dearest friend, was already there. On the king's desk was a scroll; a contract of terms that the king had signed and sealed into action. An agreement had been reached that appeased both kings without the need for war, lives lost, or surrender. They had reached a diplomatic conclusion because the other soldier, his dearest friend, had been sent as a messenger, representative of my father on behalf of both kingdoms, to reach a solution. He didn't do it for either king. He did it for his own desire of compensation, regardless of the consequences rendered to anyone else.

The new young king needed a queen in order to expand his kingdom and win favor of the people, so he propositioned my father for a deal. In exchange for my hand in marriage, the young king would not invade our kingdom or embarrass my father. He considered it a fair and kind gesture and was proud of himself for thinking of it.

When Matthew learned of the king's agreement, he immediately assembled the other knights and soldiers to make one last plea to the king for a change and permission to go to battle. Yet, no matter what he said or proposed, the king had made up his mind. Matthew wrestled with what to do. He was loyal to the king, but he was also loyal to the people he swore to protect, including me. It was as if he was being asked to choose between two things that were impossible to separate, and it filled his heart with rage and despair.

That night I fought with my father. I defied him and showed him what I really thought of him; that he was a coward and traitor to me, to his people, and to his promises that Matthew and the others had defended with their lives. I angered my father, but more than angering him, I embarrassed him and he sent me away, knowing he and I would never speak again. But that didn't solve the growing tension between my father and Matthew, who refused to give up on what he knew to be right.

My father realized that this tension with Matthew and the few soldiers and knights who stood by him wouldn't go away quietly. He knew Matthew would be a liability and a threat to his new plans. So, my father met with the other soldier that betrayed Matthew's trust one more time and devised a plan. They informed Matthew and the others that their plans for battle would be honored after all, but first, they were to be dispatched into the forest to meet with top-ranking knights and soldiers from the other kingdom, in one last effort to reach a diplomatic conclusion. It was a request and assignment that left Matthew uneasy, but he did as he was instructed.

My father and the other king, along with the help of the soldier, had made a decision that changed the course of not only that lifetime, but all the lifetimes I've lived since then, and into this lifetime now. That one decision has taken centuries to come full circle, so that all the wrongs could be made right.

That evening, as they met the other knights and soldiers in the forest, they were ambushed. Matthew was one of the few who survived and was taken prisoner into the young king's castle where he was imprisoned in a small, dark cell, which was a secret that the young king kept from me. He knew that I loved Matthew, and no matter how fairly he treated me, I did not love him. He was jealous and angered by this and it consumed him. I was the only thing he could not control or manipulate. I was the only thing that he could not attain, even though he forced me to share his bed.

Out of frustration, the young king came to me and told me that Matthew had been killed in a battle that my father had sent him into. I was devastated! However, as much as the grief overwhelmed me, I could still feel my love. He was with me everywhere I went, and it was as if he was guiding me, speaking to me, and calling out to me when he needed me. Whether or not he was a ghost to me, he felt so real. I kept looking for him outside my bedroom window, as if one day he would be there to take me home where I belonged. Little did I know that my instincts were true. He wasn't dead. He was the young king's prisoner and he was kept separated from me, even though we shared breath in the very same castle that caged us both.

At the time I was told about Matthew's supposed death, the young king learned I was pregnant and that the child wasn't his. I was pregnant with Matthew's child. I had conceived the baby right before I was sent away to be with the young king, and none of us knew of the pregnancy beforehand, not even me. But it was a child conceived in secrecy, after we eloped and married without my father's knowledge. We had planned to marry already, and chose to do it before anyone had a chance to stop us. I would have told my father, but he sent me away before I could.

Taking pride once again in his resourcefulness and kindness, the young king spared my life and offered a compromise for his generosity. He claimed the child as his own and took the opportunity to expand his lineage and build an empire that would span across history's landscape.

I lived that lifetime yearning for my true love.

Time went on and the years passed for all of us. My father died alone in his bed. The young king took his diplomacy to faraway lands and built the empire he aspired to. And I spent my life in solitude, as did my true husband who eventually died in the dark pit of isolation, several stories beneath my feet. We were so close, but still out of reach of each other, and we died searching for justice. That was, until we were born again into this lifetime.

I was 16 years old when my friends and I were at the school football game, on our way towards the concession stand. It was crowded, and we were dodging people left and right. I wasn't watching where I was going and someone bumped into my shoulder. I looked back to see a 13-year-old boy walking in the other direction. My friend said, "Did you see the way that kid was looking at you?" I did. He recognized me and I recognized him, but not in a way I could explain.

During the last couple of years of high school I bumped into him here and there, but with our age differences back then, we were worlds apart. He noticed me, though, and I remember him noticing me.

Years passed and I had my strongest awakening at the age of 24. Although I had already understood meditation, past-life memory recall, spirits, and the afterlife, it wasn't until my mid 20s that a series of events led to the realization that I had to help others with my ability to see, hear, and feel spirit.

On that path, I developed a very strong relationship with my spirit guides and meditated often. At the time, my first child, my son, was 4 years old. I was married to a man, his father, whom I loved but who did not love me back. I suffered because of it and yearned for a love I knew was possible; a love called to me from a place I couldn't describe. Here and there I would get glimpses of him, and as time went on, I started to gather information about the man I knew I would meet one day. As that happened, I also started to remember the past life you have just read about. The details came in fragments, and I learned of his smile in my visions. I could see most of his face but not enough of it to identify him completely.

A short time later I left my son's father and filed for divorce. I chose to quit my job and move "north," as my guide had suggested. I was in search of the love I saw in my visions and dreams, the love I knew I was meant to be with. My guide had instructed, "He is not here. You need to go North. Go to the hospital. That is where he is." So, my son and I moved several hours north and I began to look for a job. I had some experience as a pharmacy technician, and was positioned exactly in the middle of two hospitals that both had in-house pharmacies, along with local pharmacies positioned all around. One hospital was further north and the other was south.

Bills piled up and I had to hurry. My application at the hospital north of where I lived was declined. I was going to apply to the second hospital, but I didn't. I was concerned about the snow during the winter commute. Instead, I applied for a position at a local pharmacy and was hired.

Four short months after that, I met my second husband. He was pushy and insistent and somehow managed to completely take over my life. He joked one day that a girl he had dated used to call him "the king." She was taking down his number and asked him to spell his last name. He chuckled and said, "Okay, it's M-Y-K-I-N-G, and when she sounded it out, she looked up to see that he had gotten one over on her. Regardless, that is how he viewed himself; as a king who deserved pampering, attention, and every luxury he set his eyes on. He was born to a family that continued their lineage with every firstborn male, and he was given the same as the past three generations before him. He was the fourth of a long line of men with the same name. His father made his fortune by his own efforts, hard work, and opportunity, and he extended it to my husband when he was an older teenager. It was a relief from the poverty he had known with his mother. Before he knew it, he had everything he wanted: women, cars, money, travel, real estate, and more. He had everything he wanted except love. So when he met me and had to have me, he did everything he could to keep me and make me love him.

Within six months of being together we were fighting constantly and I knew this was something I did not want. He was controlling, and intolerant of my son. And at the time I was going to end the relationship, I believe he intentionally got me pregnant. I was trapped and wrestled with a choice: I could end the pregnancy and leave; I could keep the pregnancy and still leave; or I could keep the pregnancy and tell him about it. Telling him about the pregnancy meant I would have to stay.

Because I grew up without my father in this lifetime, I knew that I couldn't just leave and not allow my child to know his or her father. It would be criminal. Yet I grieved because I was not ready for this new baby and I felt sure he had used it as a way to keep me with him. I knew, based on my visions, that I was only going to have one more child, and that child was meant to come from the man I was meant to be with, whom I loved from long ago. But not anymore. That opportunity had been stolen from me.

Time went on and my husband and I moved west, where I had traveled and lived several times before. My second child, another son, was born. When he was 4 years old, I found my birth father. He spent his life as a pianist and traveled the world as an entertainer and astrologer. He had left my mother when she was pregnant with me, for the delight of another woman who had been their roommate. He returned to me once when I was 1 year of age but never came back for me again.

A month after I met my father, I wrote a book called *Voices Speak: A Beginner's Guide to Spirit Communication*, and he edited it as a favor. In the "special thanks" section at the beginning of the book I included an acknowledgement that reads, "To Molly and Matthew; I will see you again one day." I was feeling more and more connected to the path that would lead me to my love, and I knew I had to put this special thanks in the book, as a timestamp to show him that the memory of that lifetime was authentic and that he was who I knew he was, even if he wouldn't remember me when I finally met him.

At this time my husband received money from his father to build us a house on the property his father had purchased for us. This house was his, not mine, and I chose to stay out of any decision on what to build, what it looked like, or what type of decor he filled it with. To me, it felt like a small castle that held me prisoner with a man I didn't love. And no matter how beautiful he could make it, the house didn't mean anything to me if it was with the wrong person. I spent a lot of time in my room staring out of the window, as if someone was out there who would one day appear on the horizon to rescue me.

At that time I was completely entrenched in my medium work and spent many hours in meditation. My priority was to remote-view where my love was, and ask for guidance on what I should do next. I realized that I would have to make the necessary changes to make it happen. It was up to me, and it required every bit of faith I had. I had to trust that if I let everything go, I would be alright and so would my sons. Once again, I would have to start over in life, but that was okay. I had little attachment to anything material or physical, and I knew that if I didn't hurry, that window of time would close and I would lose the opportunity for my love and I to be reunited. Yet even though I knew he was waiting for me, he wasn't going to wait forever, and I had to act or I would lose him completely. Knowing this, and being trapped, was heartbreaking. I had no money, no freedom, and no way to escape. Not yet, anyway.

My health started to fail and I felt as if I was dying. I sought counsel from my spirit guides and was drawn to a place in meditation I had seen a thousand times; it was a field with a big oak tree, and whenever I felt I needed to connect with my guides or receive some sort of comfort, that is where I envisioned myself to be. Strangely, that vision I saw in my meditations bled into the physical world of those around me, even strangers. At one point, a man I had never known, an artist, saw a picture of my face and told me that he had seen me before in his mind and had painted me. When he sent me the images of the paintings, I was speechless. He had painted a woman with red hair who wore a flowing gown and a sad expression on her face. She was longing for her love and stood in a field near an oak tree with the setting sun behind her. He saw my memories and the place I knew to go when I needed to feel connected and at peace. I realized that this place meant more than something that had inspired my meditations, fiction, and dreams. I knew I had really been there.

Each time I envisioned myself at the tree, I slowly came to learn the full details of my past life and realized that my husband and father in this life were the kings from my past, and life was repeating history. I was in true despair and the only thing that gave me any sign of hope was the future I kept seeing for myself: being with the man in my visions and dreams. I knew if I could reach that moment, I would live and my life would be renewed. I knew that if I could reach him and *find* him, I would end the karmic cycle once and for all, and I would be able to leave both kings on *my* terms, rather than theirs.

Two years had passed and the growing tension between my father and I worsened. He wrestled with a deep guilt from the past mistakes he had made, and he often brought it into our conversations and e-mails, which created incredible tension between us. He became increasingly pushy, demanding, and overbearing, which was very unhealthy. I wanted release and resolution, not further punishment, and I found it increasingly difficult to experience a healthy relationship with him.

I reached a critical point in my life and questioned myself. Would I repeat history once again? Or would I allow myself freedom once and for all?

I made a choice. I divorced my second husband and left the marriage with nothing but a car and the clothes on my back. I also knew I would eventually have to end my relationship with my father. I didn't want anything my ex-husband had or any of the wealth his father had accumulated. All I wanted was my freedom and I was determined to have it.

That is when an opportunity came out of nowhere that made all my wishes possible. A woman contacted me who wanted to sponsor me for the work I do as a medium. She invited me to travel out of state so I could do events, group sessions, and other services. The irony was that she lived in the town next to where I grew up and attended school. It also happened to be the town that the second hospital was located in that I never applied to. Interestingly, one of her reasons for me to come there was to introduce me to a man she wanted me to meet who was like a son to her.

I had the money for the plane ticket and I was on my way. The day I met the man she wanted me to meet, my life changed. Our eyes locked and it was love at first sight. By the end of my trip, we both discovered that he had been the 13-year-old boy who had bumped my shoulder at the football game all those years ago, and we knew all the same people because we had attended the same high school and lived in the same town. I also discovered that at one point, in my mid twenties, I had lived only three doors down from where his parents have now been living for years.

He was a gentle man and I knew he was the one I had been waiting for. He had the smile I had seen in my visions, and the energy between us was incredible. His name was Matthew.

I learned that he had a fear of the dark and could not be in confined spaces. I also learned that he, too, had a past-life recall and *remembered* me, just as I had remembered him. What was most crushing was that I learned he had actually been working at the same hospital I never applied for a job at, when I was guided to go there. He was there, just as my guide had said he would be. If only I had gone to the *right* hospital, I would have met him instead of my ex-husband. However, looking at the bigger picture, it was clear that in order to resolve all of my karmic ties, I had to go through the suffering in order to come full circle back to Matthew where I belonged.

A few short months after we met, I ended the destructive relationship I had with my father, and Matthew moved west to be with me. I also stepped away from the long reach my ex-husband had on my life, even after the divorce.

A week before Matthew and I married, I received a letter from my father. At that time, he and I had been out of communication for two years. He wrote to give us his blessing for our marriage. He said he had been having dreams of us marrying and knew we must be planning it, even though he was completely unaware physically that we *had* planned it. He was sincere and spoke without harsh words, criticism, or ulterior motives. He made peace with us and since then we have all found resolution with each other.

In a phone conversation recently, my ex-husband said to me, "I knew that if you kept following the path you were on and doing the spiritual things you were doing, that you would want to be with someone else who was spiritual. And I knew that I couldn't stand in the way of it if that was your destiny." In that moment, all of my anger, frustration, and pain that I had kept with me for centuries was released. I was free, finally, of a life I had been forced to live. All of the wrongs were made right. Apologies I never thought I would receive were delivered. And I have found true freedom within. My life has completely blossomed into what I knew it would be if I only reached the lighthouse that Matthew has been for me.

Our future is no longer bound by events started long ago that needed to play out. And although the story is not over, much of the betrayal and hurt has been resolved. It is hard sometimes to see the silver lining in the gray skies of a dark time. But above those clouds is a sun that never sets in the hearts of those who keep the faith. In life there really is no death, only change. Death of the physical body does not hinder time. If love is pure, it will stand the test of time and hearts that were broken will become mended. They will see a new sunrise and find a way back to each other, just as they are meant to.

Chapter 11:
Subtle Experiences

Subtle experiences of Light happen all the time, whether we realize it or not. Beauty is constantly revealed by Spirit, as are little messages leading us on the pathway of our destiny.

As I started putting together *The Light*, and soon after my spiritual awakening, I kept seeing the numbers 3, 33, and 333. I would see these number combinations daily, and often. When I looked at the time it would be 3:33 or 11:33; on restaurant bills I'd notice that the total had come to €33.33; in supermarkets fruits and vegetables were 33 cents a kilo; numbers on doors and number-plates contained the numbers 333; and the list continues. But the real loud and clear message came after I had started to form a relationship with my now-husband, Terry Tillman. The relationship felt different than relationships I had shared with other men. The connection between us felt deeper, as if we had known each other for several lifetimes. I often felt that I knew exactly what he was thinking, and I felt a constant and pure, unconditional Love for him.

At first our relationship was long-distance, as he lived in Los Angeles, California, and I lived in Malaga, Spain. We would see each other once every few months, and in between time we would send each other daily text messages and e-mails, and skype every now and again. On one particular day, we hadn't spoken for some time, so we had a lot of catching up to do. We spoke for hours, and then, feeling exhausted (as by now it was the early hours in the morning in Spain), I said that I had better go to bed. We always spent at least five or 10 minutes saying goodbye, neither one of us wanting to be the first to end the call.

When we finally did press the little red button to cut off the call, I immediately noticed how long the call had lasted: 3 hours, 33 minutes, and 33 seconds. It was at that point that a knowing shot into my heart, telling me all I needed to know—Terry and I would be together on a long-term basis, and later we would get married.

A year or so later, when I went to the U.S. Embassy in London to get a six-month visa for America, the ticket I was handed had the number 333 printed on it. I'd felt a little worried that my visa would be denied, but when I saw that number, I knew everything would be just fine. And it was.

I could tell you literally hundreds of stories of my own subtle experiences of the Light, but instead, read the following stories, and see if you remember any of your own. I'll bet that you can think of at least a few!

KRISS ERICKSON
Reiki Master
Everett, Washington, United States

Love Comes Out On Top

I both loved and hated Butler, New Jersey, the tiny town where I grew up. In many ways it was easier to hate it—not just the town but the people too, and the hierarchical structure, especially the unquestionable authority of the people I called "mother" and "father." As I grew, the things that urged me to hate my parents' house outpaced the things I loved, but the things I loved were in many ways stronger, since they formed a foundation that set a freer tone for my adult life.

One of the first things I learned to love about Butler, New Jersey were the small creatures that shared space with us humans. In the summer, flies would land on grass stems to shed their skins, leaving behind perfect crystalline molds of their former, smaller selves. I used to lie in the grass, which rarely got mowed, and watch the flies land. I'd cup my hand over my mouth so that my breath wouldn't disturb the tiny insects as they split their too-small skins and stepped out, buzzing their shiny new wings as they flew into the blue sky. I loved to watch the flies because I felt like my own skin was too small. I wished that all it would take for me as a human to step into a new life would be to split my too-tight skin—the skin that was defined by both parents, beaten by my father's fists, and whipped with forsythia branches wielded by my mother—and fly away to a new life.

Eastern toads were another example of a creature that inspired love. For 10 months out of the year there was no indication that toads lived anywhere near our tiny town. But at the end of July, a parade of toads of all sizes, from hatchlings barely big enough to hop to experienced migrators, would suddenly appear. They hopped across streets and sidewalks, showed up in gardens, and made lawns their temporary highway.

While I didn't question the appearance of the toads in my childhood, I eventually learned that people had built towns and roads across their ancient migration territory. All I knew as a child was that I loved their bulging eyes and their gentle acceptance when I cupped them in my hands. I kept several as pets, learning that they were resourceful enough to be able to catch flies in their terrarium home and to burrow into the flowerbox outside my bedroom window for the winter.

The first year that I kept toads over the winter, when my mother insisted I put the amphibians outside, I worried that they would freeze and that I'd never see them again. Even the threat of a beating as a result of my squeals of joy didn't stop me from expressing my elation when I saw my beloved pets emerge from the mud the following spring. How I wished I could be like the toads, appearing and disappearing as my inner wisdom led, not being tied down to the dreary little clapboard house and the backward-thinking town.

Don't get me wrong—I'm not slamming the whole town. I'm pointing out a limited way of thinking that meant ignoring abuse, insisting that children who dared to "defy" their parents by reporting abuse were liars, and a general attitude that commiserated with parents when their sons and daughters "forced" them to hit, yell at, or demean them.

Given the environment of enforced silence, books were another of my great loves. In many ways, books gave me a deeper sense of salvation than the creatures I loved. One of the few kind things my mother shared was an appreciation for classic fiction. When my father decided that his family would join a restrictive cult, which meant no activity of any kind on the "Sabbath," my mother read Jack London's *Call of the Wild* or Felix Salten's *Bambi*. In the words of those books I found truths that were bigger than the things my parents and hometown urged me to believe. In Jack London's words I found courage in the face of danger and the truth that each being on this planet has the right to defend him- or herself. In Felix Salten's words I discovered the truth that it isn't weak to love or be loved.

From that foundation, I discovered Albert Payson Terhune, a New Jersey author who wrote of his deep love for dogs. I dove into the works of Pearl S. Buck, who spoke of the Chinese people: their courage, their families, human nature, and how our choices shape our lives. From the words of these and many other authors, I was able to do something my parents never intended me to do: formulate my own ideas about how the world worked and why I was in it.

I began writing, expressing my voice in silent, passionate words that spoke of the horrors of being woken after midnight to vicious parental arguments that could climax with my father thundering up the stairs to express his frustration by beating one of his children. I spoke of the intense hunger I'd felt hundreds of times after my mother decided I needed to be punished so I was not permitted to eat. Sometimes, she'd make me watch the rest of the family eat. Other times, she simply sent me to bed without dinner—an accepted form of punishment in the 1950s and '60s.

Because my parents were smart people, they made sure that anything I expressed, through words, writing, or any other means, would be viewed as fiction. And because I read so much fiction, my written and spoken words were seen as fiction by teachers and others who intervened. But through expressing myself I was able to bleed off some of the internalized fear, stagnation, and anger that resulted from being a ping pong ball at the whim of my parents' anger.

A third thing I loved about Butler New Jersey was singing. Even though the cult my father had forced us to join didn't allow us to keep traditional holidays like Christmas, for some reason I was allowed to be in choir throughout grade and high school. We didn't have a middle school, just grades K through eight in elementary school and nine through 12 in high school. Our fourth-grade choir director, Mr. Zinc, had big dreams. He'd play records of professional child singers for us to listen to. "Hear the passion in that tone!" he'd cry. Then he'd urge, "Now you try it!" And we did. Some of us got the message—that by focusing our feelings into the tones produced by our voices, we could convey concepts that went well beyond words.

I learned that when I sang the descant in the *Battle Hymn of the Republic* not only was I focusing on the ideals of courage, freedom, and justice, but I was able to express some of my own yearnings for those things as well. There were many other things I loved about Butler, New Jersey, in the '50s, '60s, and '70s. I loved the streams that ran so clear and clean that brook and rainbow trout grew fat and healthy. I loved the black snakes and garter snakes that sunned themselves on granite shelves. I loved the woodland trail behind the bargain market that led to the town library. I loved how the town park was lit up each year for Christmas. I even loved the cemetery, with its mix of tombstones from the 1700s through the 1970s, reminding me that life is a cycle. Even at the worst parts of any given life, the darkness is a precursor for light and renewed life.

And that's how the light won out in my life. All of the elements that I learned to love showed me that my parents had chosen their dark paths. They'd chosen to treat their children harshly, and that in turn led to them spending the last years of their lives in misery and loneliness. At the same time, all of the small things that I learned to love led me to create a path full of Light.

STEPHEN SERETAN
Teacher of the KISS Releasing System
Los Angeles, California, United States

My Life-Changing Miracle

I have had many unusual experiences in the Light. They have increased in number since working with a true Master for 11 years, beginning in 1983. His name was Lester Levenson, and I practiced his technique called KISS Releasing. But even before that, the Light blessed me with events that can only be described as miraculous. One such event was indeed life-transforming. It made me a devotee of the Light forever, and proved to me that we are truly under the watchful care and love of an invisible Divine presence.

I am a film composer and had just scored the music for the pilot of a TV series called *The Paper Chase* in 1977. It was going to be sold for the 1977/78 season on CBS. Out of 200 pilots, it was picked up for 22 episodes, and I was to be the composer for the entire run. The founder and CEO of CBS, William S. Paley, loved the show and was an old friend of the star, industry legend John Houseman. He was the co-writer of Orson Welles's masterpiece *Citizen Kane*, and a producer-director of many films in the 1940s and '50s. *The Paper Chase* film, however, was his first foray as an actor. He was the perfect choice for the role of Charles Kingsfield, the infamous Contract Law professor at Harvard Law School.

I was hired to score the pilot by my manager, who produced the feature film. CBS loved my music, as did Houseman, so I was off and running. However, darkness approached to blot out my victory and remove me from the show. The studio executives feared the public would turn off this high-level drama about life in an Ivy League Law school, so they began to monkey with the show. The producer (and my ally) was fired and a less-qualified man was brought in. I was devastated. My short-lived music career was over. Or so I thought.

I felt very low and depressed, and I did the only thing I could do. I turned within. Every night before sleep I would read a section from a little booklet called *Metaphysical Meditations*, by the great Indian master Parmahansa Yogananda. He was the first real Master to live in America and started the Self Realization Fellowship here in the 1920s. I had visited one of his temples in Pacific Palisades and had bought the book years earlier. Little did I know what this small tome would reveal to me. I have since discovered that even the smallest actions can create ripples that cause waves of change in one's life.

After one month of this homespun spiritual "sadhana," the Light blessed me. My agent called and said that, with a few weeks to go before shooting the pilot, they had no production script ready. My manager was rehired, something that almost *never* happens in Hollywood. I was back on the show for the entire run. Houseman even invited me to lunch in the studio commissary, which was a thrilling experience.

This was to become a monumental turn of events, because the series was then brought back to be the first American TV series ever to be produced for cable. It was on Showtime when cable networks were just coming onto the scene. It helped make that network into the powerhouse it is today, and the show is still highly regarded by all of Hollywood. I was the composer for the three years it ran on Showtime, and I had an unforgettable experience. It played all over the world and I received fan mail for my contribution. It seems that film music *is* listened to even though it is in the background.

The Light brought the seemingly deceased body of my music career back to life. My work on that series is still helping me today as a highly regarded credit. I am forever grateful to the Light.

PAUL HUNTING

Founder and Director of Horsejoy Authentic Leadership
Stratford-upon-Avon, United Kingdom

The Trunk Call from Spirit

Thirty years ago I had an experience of how powerful the Light truly is. I have no idea why it gave me this gift. Perhaps it was telling me it was bigger than me, bigger than my mind, bigger than all of time and space. I still don't know.

I find it easy enough to comprehend—on a verbal level—that time is an illusion. We can grasp the concept that the only reality is the now. Mystics and sages through the ages continue to say this and elaborate upon it.

This implies that if everything was created in the beginning, the past and the future are as one. It's tough to swallow, but are the future and the past simply revealing themselves like timed-release vitamins? The future, perhaps—but the past too? If so, is it possible for something to happen in the past that could only have happened in the future?

Through the agency of the light, I have learned that *anything* is possible.

In my early teens, having spent a decade or so being frightened and punished in God's name, I at last felt safe enough to declare myself an atheist. In many ways I still am. I don't believe in God, I simply know now through direct, unshakeable, personal experience that there's "something" transcendent in the universe that is totally, unconditionally loving, and infinitely mischievous that unfailingly brings me exquisite joy when I tap into it.

When I was born I was originally called Vicram. My Jewish mother and soon-to-be absent father were members of a yogic community called Shanti Sedan. I remember little about this. My father left home. My mother adored me. She called me Paul and spoiled me rotten.

As an adult, in December 1978, I bought a very large aluminum trunk. I stuffed all of my possessions into it and locked it shut. Somehow I wrestled it down to the basement of the apartment building where I lived. It fleetingly occurred to me that this was some kind of metaphor. But little did I know then what my stuff would be transformed into, and what sequence of seemingly random events and coincidences would happen to transform my consciousness. My downstairs friend and neighbor, Susannah, promised to safeguard the trunk until I returned. I rented out my flat, promised my girlfriend I'd be faithful, and flew to Auckland, New Zealand, where I had been given a dream job as head of copywriting. I'd left my job at Saatchi & Saatchi in London for Masius, in Auckland, and I thought I was now firmly on the path to success—meaning sunshine, fast cars, no more rush-hour tubes, and a beach at the end of the garden.

One fine day, I was driving at high speed into the countryside when, contrary to my normal selfish inclinations, I picked up a hitchhiker. He told me he was going to an annual event called Nambassa—a huge pop festival up north with a smaller healing festival attached. "A healing festival?" I asked.

"Why don't you come along and see?" he asked. "No way," I said. "Not my thing at all."

But a seed had been planted. The truth was, as soon as he had said it I felt the urge to go. But pride and fear stopped me. How could I begin to admit how empty I felt, despite my outward success?

Throughout that year things got so bad that I made a conscious choice to give up my atheism. I knew one or two people who were following an unorthodox spiritual path and I envied their relaxed happiness. I decided simply to be open to the possibility of "something else" and see what happened. I had little to lose.

Twelve months later, like a fish on a line, I was reeled in to Nambassa. I found myself listening to a guru, Swami Satchidananda, addressing the multitude. He looked just how God is supposed to—long white hair, flowing beard, and a soft smile radiating love and peace.

The next day, I sniffed cautiously round the healing festival. I sat on the grass before a panel of speakers lined up on the stage. One introduced himself with, "My name's John, and I'm a disciple of Jesus Christ." My stomach churned. Later, some hippy-looking American dude called Jonathan got up and said something that made perfect sense. An hour or so later I was sitting bemused and shy in what he called an "American Indian Healing Circle." I had no idea what to expect.

An hour or so later I was floating back to my tent two feet above the ground. I was in a pure state of bliss and unconditional love. Not only was I higher than I'd ever been, but I knew that something inside me was doing this; something real, natural, and powerful. It was also free—and legal!

Two days later, I was down to earth again with a crash. I resolved not to take another breath until I could access that place myself, at will, and live my life from it. But I had no real idea what it was or how to find it, and soon the blissful state of being I had found was as elusive as ever. But as the tragi-comedy of my life unfolded, it seemed "it" was looking for me as much as I "it." It didn't look like it at the time, but a long series of nudges, jolts, and weird coincidences ushered me into a greater destiny and a much greater sense of inner fulfillment.

Of course, in hindsight, it's easy to say this. Looking back at the dots, it's as easy to connect them into a constellation. It's easy to read a superconscious will into a random series of unconnected coincidences, directing the traffic of events. To the skeptical mind, what you need is foresight. The trouble is, if we know the future before it shows up we're unlikely to go through the tests necessary to make it happen. But suppose you travel back into the past and see the future in the present? Wouldn't that be cool? Well, that's exactly what did happen.

I followed Jonathan around like a lost puppy for several months, never even remotely hitting that delicious spot again. Then, while out riding horses, it was as if a karmic hand pushed me off my horse. Instead of rolling, I stuck out my hand with the futility of a King Canute, and broke my wrist. At this time my birthday was coming up, and as a gift to my girlfriend, I took my broken wrist in its cast back home to England. It was to be a surprise visit. The surprise, however, was on me.

Her new boyfriend.

Rejected and dejected, I found myself at the World Symposium on Humanity, a huge international event linking by satellite fellow seekers of Truth in London, Los Angeles, and Toronto. Through remarkable serendipity, I found myself once again listening to the same ubiquitous Swami. The irony of the journey from Saatchi & Saatchi to Satchidananda did not escape me.

After the panel discussion, I queued up to say hello.

The Chair was also chatting to folks in the queue and I caught her eye. I was still painfully shy, but I think I may have squeezed out a smile. We got to talking. She thrust a piece of paper at me and said, "Darlink, you must come to my say-me-narrah," in a heady, Mediterranean accent. It was an offer I could not refuse. I read the brochure. It could have been written just for me. "First I'll go back to New Zealand," I said. "I have a job. I'll come back in June, okay?"

"Darlink," she said, "if you go home, you won'ta come back."

I knew inside that she was right. I was learning about trust and surrender. It was thrilling to just "let go and let God." And so I resigned—just like that! By some miracle, I found enough freelance copywriting work in London to pay for my keep and for the "say-me-narrah."

It was, in fact, the first UK Insight Seminar, in June 1979. I got to spend five days with some truly amazing folks, including John-Roger. J-R, as he likes to be called, was facilitating the event from the back of the room. I emerged on day six floating on a cloud, 10 feet above ground. (Note: this is eight feet higher than after Nambassa). I had found what I had been looking for— and then some. More accurately, I had found myself! Apart from clearing out a lot of old inner junk, I learned I had the power of free choice—the freedom to choose not only my actions, but also my inner responses to life's slings and arrows. I was learning to choose my inner experience regardless of external circumstances. I was also learning the inner pathway to my source of bliss, and ultimate liberation.

The next two years brought one spontaneous adventure after another—too varied to detail. I had been a dead man walking for many years, so I had to make up for lost time. I gave no thought whatsoever to my huge locked trunk in my friend's basement. I oscillated between New Zealand, Los Angeles, and Sydney as the mood or the money took me.

I had fallen hopelessly in love with the people and the committed spiritual lifestyle in L.A. My atheism had been an important phase in my spiritual evolution, but now I was absolutely going for the highest experience of soul awareness I could muster. A major part of my life was now studying the teachings of John-Roger. The two key processes this involves are spiritual exercises (SEs)—which is like meditation—and reading discourses. While the SEs are practiced ideally for two hours each day, the discourses are little booklets with information on a myriad of spiritual topics—from working with the light to karma, responsibility, and the Philosopher's Stone. There are 144 of these to be read, one a month for 12 years of study. Back then, each booklet would arrive in the post every month. It was always a treat to open the manila envelope to see what sacred subject would be covered in J-R's inimitable style.

By the time I returned to the UK and reclaimed my flat, I was on discourse 18 or so. This was late 1981.

The time came to release the last remnants of my past self buried in the monster trunk. But something mysterious and remarkable was about to happen. When I finally lugged this thing up to my flat and lifted the lid, on the very top of the contents was something that could not possibly be there. Had my future self traveled back to my past and simply winked at me in the present? There it was: a brand-new, crisp, untouched, pristine discourse! It was blue. The title was "Discipline." It was from midway through year five. How on earth did it get there? How could a real, physical object, a booklet written by J-R, be in a trunk I had locked three years before I'd even heard of J-R, let alone read his discourses?

Thirty years have now passed since that discovery. I have no rational explanation. I am still working with the profound inner message it stamped indelibly on my consciousness.

GLENN MOORE
Life Coach and Spiritual Teacher
United Kingdom

Living My Passion

The elderly couple alongside me held hands. To my left, rolling fields replicated to a tree-lined and ever-expanding horizon. I was on a train, returning home. And I loved the views.

Two years earlier, I left the office of my law firm for the last time. On that day, the sun shone in a deep blue sky and I received several text messages of support: "Hello, oh free one! What a beautiful day to be free!" And on the way home, I found a £20 note.

That morning I had a vivid dream of the hanging man from the Tarot. Fearing the worst, I was reassured to read from my dream dictionary that the situation might look negative but it is actually positive. Everything was falling beautifully into place.

One "blip," as it seemed at the time, was the sudden apparent failure of my cell phone. I went to a local shop, and in less time than it would have taken me to send a two-line text, a pretty lady handed back my handset, fully functional again. She smiled knowingly as I left. And so it began.

Jumping Off the Cliff

For 28 years, I had lived and breathed being a lawyer, and now I had nothing planned to replace it. I had money in the bank, but I was about to have no income. I had examined and thought through several conceivable worst-case scenarios, including bankruptcy and even suicide. Thankfully, more positive thoughts appeared concerning what I might do, but nothing made my heart, or any other part of me, sing.

"You're mad," said one of my friendlier partners when I told him of my departure and nonexistent plans. I laughed, but also thought, *God, have I done the "right" thing?* My friend later confided that he would do the same if he didn't need to pay the mortgage and his daughter's school fees! Still, his first reaction came back to me many times as I ventured into the unknown, especially during the moments of doubt.

"You've jumped off of the cliff," said a close friend. I laughed again. My mind was already seeing the dark side but I kept telling myself that I had done the right thing. Instinctively, I knew that I had to stop listening to my mind and start following my heart. Putting this into practice was much harder than I had anticipated, yet I set the intent.

Practicing law for an international shipping practice gave me travel, prestige, and abundant material wealth, but little peace, harmony, or spiritual well-being. Drawn like neglected iron filings to a more nurturing magnet, I tried to redress the imbalance by reading as many spiritual and personal development books as I could during the modicum of "me time" I had available. Now that I had all the "me time" I could possibly want, or so it seemed, a plethora of unread books fell, sometimes literally, from creaking shelves and window sills into my hands.

One such book was *Synchronicity: The Inner Path of Leadership* by Joe Jaworski. He was another lawyer who had left a successful law firm to do something completely different. He had been drawn to a spiritual path, and was now writing about the synchronicities that had helped or guided him. I resonated with almost everything he had written, as if I was reading my own story, of the past as well as of a prospective future. One afternoon, I was focused on some of Joe's "tests, trials, and ordeals." Minutes later I completely overreacted to an e-mail from the office concerning a case I had not been able to conclude. I, too, was now being tested. Mentally and emotionally I had not yet fully let go!

My former life clung to me for a long while. Or perhaps I clung to it? I had repeated, though not recurring, dreams, about my former partners and other colleagues. Two months or so into my new life, I attended a sort of end-of-school celebration with my tantric group. As the evening was about to close, we all picked a heart card from a double deck. I chose "Surrender," with the subtext, "Let go and all will be fine." The message was clear but its realization seemed to be blocked.

"Some seeds will fall on stony ground. Others will grow and flourish," said a voice. This was to presage yet more tests of letting go and trusting that all would be fine. Silver linings appeared. Relieved of some but not all of my old work-related thinking, I could more easily open to the subtle messages and nuances of life around me. I started journaling, which brought me to a greater awareness of my inner and outer worlds. I assiduously recorded messages from several sources. Guidance came mostly from books, but also from films and songs. I could now marvel at some of the incredible wisdom emanating from everyday material that had most often passed me by, usually because my mind was "too busy." Hearing the Beatles sing *Let it Be* in a quieter moment stopped me completely in my tracks after a particularly raw day of criticizing myself, the world, and almost everything in it. The next day I was reading *The Power of Coincidences* by David Richo and the following words jumped out of the page: "In the course of life we are wise to be ready for the many unexpected characters crossing our path..."

Easing the Pain

I love waterfalls. There is an especially spectacular fall at Pistyll Rhaeadr in the UK's Berwyn Mountains. It is the highest natural waterfall in Wales, and I had arranged to meet a friend of a friend there. I sat for a while, alone on a small tree-trunk bench, some way back from the waterfall, and within a few yards of the outdoor café where my friend was working, waiting to take her break. I became aware of a white-haired man with a stick approaching me. He sat tentatively alongside me and introduced himself as Alex. He was visiting too, he explained. He said he loved the energy there. I told him about some workshops I had been running and shared what I had learned of the healing powers of water, especially standing under a waterfall. He said he too had learned a little about healing. He had suffered a great deal of physical pain in his earlier life but had found a solution.

"By breathing intently into the area of pain, I could dissolve it," he said.

"Well, you look pretty well on it," I said.

"How old do you think I am?" he asked, grinning impishly. I guessed 70. "I am 92," he said. "I used to cycle and swim every day of my life until I was 80! And I was a singer too." He was also blind!

The Problem Is the Mind

Two years later, I was attending the Oneness University in India and one of the teachers there repeated almost exactly what the blind man had said about dissolving pain. And I have used it on myself many times since.

Not earning, and spending days doing nothing at all—or at least nothing productive in the conventional sense—brought up a lot of fear and self-doubt. Underlying all fears is a lack of trust in ourselves, I read in another book. Part of me could still not trust that I had made the right decision. My mind seemed to constantly nag and nudge me.

"You're doing nothing," it said, or "you *should* be doing something," or, "you're doing the 'wrong' thing." To the judgmental mind, nothing I could do would ever be good enough. Yet I could see that none of the internal moaning and complaining made any difference at all to what was or wasn't happening around me. What was really causing me stress was my thinking. What was happening "out there" was just fine. The "problem" was inside me, in my mind!

There came a point when I had spent virtually all of my savings and was earning only modest amounts from coaching. This created more anxiety. Again, the real cause was my thinking, in believing the situation to be "bad," irreversible, or worse! And when I stopped and listened more closely to the nagging voice, there came another revelation: It was not me talking at all, but my parents! I was hearing their words and voices in my head—even my father's tone of voice. It was like playing an old record. *But, hold on*, I thought, *I am not them and they are not me! So who is "me" and who or what is doing the thinking?*

Now for the Bigger Picture

Back at the Oneness University, I was in the audience listening to a Q&A session and someone asked the $64,000 question: "Who or what is the 'I'?" The answers seemed vague, or maybe they just went over my head. Oneness was mentioned, along with the phrase "I am that I am," which was a completely new concept to me. Then someone said, "There is only one mind, a universal mind." Ergo, it was misleading or even delusional to speak of "my mind" or "your mind." This did not resonate with me at all.

Back home, I was drawn to another book. I had read Eckhart Tolle's *The Power of Now* in my old life and thought I had taken it all in, but the essence must have completely escaped me because it felt as if I was reading the book for the first time. The answers seemed to pour from the pages as if they were meant exclusively for me! I saw that much of my past, my beliefs, my thinking, and my behavior had been driven by one source: ego, or the false self! In time, as I began to recognize it in action, I realized that I could rise above it and see a bigger picture, like watching myself on stage from an audience. There was, it seemed, always something behind ego behavior. And that something was the realization of a far greater reality and a new potential to life. I was becoming aware of another, more authentic me behind the ego mask.

I decided to take a road trip through the United States. I chose to fly into Seattle, then drive Vancouver (Washington) and then Phoenix. Other than Vancouver Island and Sedona, I had not planned any specific intermediate ports of call. I would go wherever life took me. I had a few American friends living in Washington, Oregon, and California whom I could visit, but that was it. As the journey progressed and as I allowed it to happen, I was open to other guidance.

I had more unread books in my travel bag. One "called" me to Ashland, another to Mount Shasta. The latter had the greater draw, though I checked in on Ashland too. The views from Mount

Shasta were spectacular. I decided to hike up it as high as I could go. From the parking area, I followed a broad path flanked intermittently by heavy boulders. As it narrowed and became steeper, a small squirrel-type rodent and several birds appeared ahead. Climbing higher, the path suddenly disappeared, so I followed a blackbird up to a partially leveled section with smaller flat-topped stones. On one of these stood a rough-edged rock, jet-black and shaped uncannily like the mountain itself. There, perched alongside it, was my guide-bird! I knew the rock was meant for me.

On the ascent, so far as I could see, I was the only soul on the mountain. At one point, about an hour into the climb, I sensed someone standing on the ridge, a few yards away, to the right and above me. I stopped and stared at what my visual faculty told me was empty space, but a sixth sense felt that something or someone was there. Perhaps it was an entity or spirit.

My mind was increasingly opening to reality beyond the five senses. The Mount Shasta incident reinforced this. I read more and more about the invisible world—a world of energy fields, past lives, angels, spirit guides, and other-dimensional beings. Despite my very traditional background, these other realities were entirely plausible to me, even to my ego mind. In fact, as my discoveries and awareness expanded, I felt I was gaining a distinct inner knowing of reality beyond the conventional world of "what you see is all there is." I saw films like *The Matrix* in a whole new light as I embraced quantum physics. There are seven words in *The Matrix* that powerfully illustrate the difference between thinking or believing something, often what we have been taught to believe by others, and an inner knowing that carries absolute certainty: "Don't think you are, *know* you are..." For me, this is a literal expression of the totality, from where everything is possible. But we must know it. It's much more than a thought or a belief. It's a transition to a new reality, from doing and thinking, to being, where there can be no limits on speed or anything else in the material world. It is about knowing our own true self and potential, what many call the Higher Self. My intent is to know this Higher Self and to be it.

The Power of Passion

My *Sharing Your Passion* video series was inspired by a similarly empowering film about an impossible dream. But the dreamer knew only "possible." It is an overwhelming and audacious story of the triumph of spirit over matter, of truth over doubt, and of love over fear. In the film I saw genuine, unconditional passion and an exquisite love for the gift that one man had come to give to the world. I cried, sobbed even, as this man's greatest supporter and accomplice broke down in tears at the deeper realization of the emotional enormity of what they had achieved. The film emerged at a time when many people, including myself, were being called to find and live their true passion. The film is called *Man on Wire* and the dreamer is Philippe Petit, who walked a tightrope rigged between the Twin Towers of New York not once but eight times, 450 meters above the ground. Why? As Petit himself expressed it, "There is no why!" It was his passion. No explanation necessary. I had not even heard of Petit before watching this film. I was at a friend's house one weekend waiting for her and her husband to get ready to go out when I picked up a magazine to pass the time. I don't read magazines but I opened it at the very page of this article. And I devoured it avidly. Of course, I had to see the film. It occurred to me that there must be hundreds of people like Petit, who are not as well-known, whom we may never see or hear about on television or in the newspapers, but who are living their passion in such a way that they can inspire others. When I asked my first guest to be interviewed for *Sharing My Passion* and he said yes, and then the next one said yes, and so on, I knew this was what I was meant to do. I could now unconditionally trust that I had done the "right" thing. My train has passed through several tunnels. There are stations to come, more fields, more trees, and more views to love. And the horizon keeps on expanding.

Chapter 12:
Out-of-Body Experiences

I recall something frightening happening on several occasions when I was a child. I would wake up in the middle of the night with a loud buzzing sound in my ears, and my whole body was paralyzed. I fought to move and couldn't. The buzzing would get louder and louder, and I would become and more desperate to move. I felt totally out of control over whatever these vibrations were. Finally, I would fight them off with my willpower, the buzzing sound would disappear, and I'd be left with a rapidly beating heart and a sweaty body.

As I grew older, and after reading the book *Journeys out of the Body* by Robert Munroe, I began to realize that these vibrations had been the beginnings of an out-of-body experience. Curious, and at that point ready to explore other realms, I decided that the next time it happened, I would mentally tell myself, "Take me to my Higher Self." The vibrations started about two nights later, as if I had opened a door, welcoming an out-of-body experience to take place. This time, I totally surrendered and did not fight it away. I completely let go, and I began to feel my Light body sinking down into the mattress, and then to the wooden frame of the bed. That in itself was a strange experience, as I felt the denseness of the mattress, and then the even denser wooden frame, packed tight with molecules. At that point I remembered that ideally I wanted to rise up, not sink down, so I told myself the mental command, "Take me to my Higher Self."

Almost instantly, my body began shooting upwards, through a kaleidoscopic collection of colors, patterns, and Light, until I reached a tunnel, which was not more than three meters high, with a white floor and a white ceiling. Towards the end of the tunnel, I noticed a mirror and felt shocked when I saw myself in it. I was completely naked and I saw how my Light body looked exactly the same as my physical body, even down to the mole in the center of my torso. I also realized that I was floating in mid-air, and I felt free, too—an amazing sense of freedom that I will never forget. Around the corner, I saw two doors and I felt nervous about what I might find inside either door, but I took the risk and opened one of them. Inside, there was an office-like atmosphere and a lady sitting behind a desk working on her computer. "How can I help?" she asked. Suddenly I felt extremely embarrassed, knowing that I was stark naked, while she was dressed in a smart office uniform. There were also two young men behind the desk, chewing on straws and drinking water, but I feel sure that I wasn't visible to them, as they paid no attention and did not even look up.

I told the lady, "I've left my body back on my bed at home, and I don't know where I am." She looked at me knowingly and said, "Ahhh, so you're one of them..." Later, I realized that she meant I was an out-of-body explorer, or an astral traveler. The conversation continued for a few more minutes, and then I heard a whooshing sound and felt myself land back into my body on the bed, with a jolt.

Throughout the following nights, I had more out-of-body experiences, each with a different story, similar but not the same. Months later, the night after I finally committed to go on a wilderness trip, facilitated by Terry Tillman (who is now my husband, and who has shared a few of his own Light experiences in this book), I had another out-of-body experience, this time very different. I awoke in the middle of the night, again to the buzzing sounds and powerful vibrations, and saw a being hovering above me. He stretched his arms down and pulled my Light body out of my physical body. The being leaned on my back, guiding us as we floated through the cosmos, passing through walls and structures. It was all a pleasurable blur of color and Light. I did not feel afraid; rather, I felt that this being was part of me—as if I had come home. We suddenly arrived at a lake. It was a beautifully sunny day and there were lots of people by the side of the lake, engaging in various summer activities. The being placed me down on a rowing boat and then left me for a while. I floated peacefully on the lake feeling submerged in bliss and joy. After a while, the being collected me again and we took off, heading back towards my bed, where he finally lowered my Light body back inside my physical body. During that process, I had the most amazing full-body orgasm, which left me feeling exhilarated and deeply relaxed.

Now, fast-forward five weeks. I flew from Malaga, Spain, to Boise, Idaho, where a wilderness trip would begin. From there we boarded a small bus, which took us through the small town of Stanley, and finally to Redfish Lake. At the lake we would get on two boats to take us to the starting point of our hike into the Sawtooth Mountains. As the bus weaved around little mountain roads en route to the lake, I was talking to another two participants on the trip about déjà vu, and we shared stories. As the bus turned off the road, and drove along the alley leading to Redfish

Lake, I suddenly had the most profound experience of déjà vu, and I told the people I was talking to and laughed, finding that really peculiar. But nothing could prepare me for what I saw around the next corner... There was Redfish Lake, and it was the very lake that I had visited in my out-of-body experience; the very lake that the mysterious being had taken me to! I froze, feeling shocked for some time, before I finally had to tell someone. It's no coincidence that I chose to tell Terry. As the 10-day trip in the Sawtooth Mountains unfolded, I could tell that there was a spark of chemistry between Terry and me, and there were untold synchronicities. I knew we would be together, even though there had been no obvious signs that he liked me, and despite the fact that I now know there were 38 years between us.

Later, as our romance blossomed, I discovered that it had been Terry who had taken me out of my body that night. His Light body had come to show my Light body where we would be spending 10 days!

And as if all that wasn't enough, when I went to McAllen, Texas, to do my first speaking event at the Infinite Love charity, a psychic lady offered me a free reading. She spoke a lot about Terry and I, and she said that we had been together in many lifetimes before this one. She said that previously we had shared a life together in the Sawtooth Mountains. I had not mentioned anything about the Sawtooth Mountains to her, so this came as a complete surprise, and I smiled inside, as all the pieces of the jigsaw puzzle finally started to fit together.

I've told several people about my out-of-body experiences, and it always amazes me how many of us have left our physical bodies, but haven't wanted to tell anyone due to fear of being ridiculed or not believed.

Following are more stories of out-of-body experiences—it's probably no surprise that one of them is written by Terry!

TRICIA GABBITAS
Poet and Songwriter, Retired Secretary
North Yorkshire, United Kingdom

At the age of 12, I had my appendix removed. Unfortunately, unknown to the surgeon, I had a slight abnormality—a small bulge on the intestines. During the surgery, my intestines became twisted around it. I was rushed to hospital and ultimately taken to the operating theater where it was discovered that my intestines had died and I had gangrene inside. The surgeon removed half of my intestines and I was dangerously ill for days and not expected to live.

I was in my hospital bed with the curtains drawn, totally obscuring the surrounding views, when I found myself floating above my body in the bed. I saw the curtains all around my bed and I saw the nurse at the end of the ward, sitting at the desk with a small lamp beside her. All I felt was peace. No fear, no worries. I don't recall returning to my body, but I survived against all the odds. From the age of 13 I discovered a gift for writing poetry and have written hundreds since, many of which are Christian poems.

TERRY TILLMAN
Leadership Seminar Leader, Motivational Speaker
Scout, Ketchum, Idaho, United States

Ever since I was a little boy I've been fascinated with the Great Pyramid and the Giza Plateau in Cairo, Egypt. In my 20s and 30s I read a few books about Egypt, and as the years passed I grew increasingly fascinated with the subject. In meditation I received information that's contrary to what's written in the books. For example, the history books say the pyramids were a burial place for the pharaohs, but no one has ever found a mummy in a pyramid. The Valley of Kings is the real burial place of the Pharaohs. The books say the Great Pyramid was built by 50,000 slaves with inclines and pulleys, but there is no evidence of that either. I knew that the Egyptians had the ability to make solid objects malleable, and they could levitate large stones by using energy.

In 1979 I went on a cruise to see the Cheops Pyramid with a group of spiritual teachers and a friend named Cara. Inside, there are two famous rooms: the Queen's Chamber and the King's Chamber. I was more interested in seeing the King's Chamber, but first we were led into the Queen's Chamber. Our facilitator claimed to have the keys to unlocking the energy so we could experience the full power of the pyramid. To get there we had to crawl through an approximately 6-foot-wide, 4-foot-tall tunnel that opened up into the room. I made sure I was the last one in so I would be first out to continue on to the King's Chamber.

In the Queen's Chamber we did a chant and meditation, and as I wanted to get to the King's Chamber before anyone else, I hurried out of the exit when the time came to leave. First I came to the ascending passage with the grand gallery, a huge stairway with handrails that enters the pre-room, or the antechamber. Before I was about to duck down to enter the antechamber I heard a sound, which was a cross between a flute and people chanting, but not quite either one. It was a little eerie, yet at the same time, harmonious, enticing, and irresistible. I wondered what was going on. I ducked into the King's Chamber, and there before my eyes I saw that everyone from my group was already in there, chanting. I wondered how they had gotten there before me. I was positive that I had been the first to leave the Queen's Chamber, and there was only one route to reach the King's Chamber.

I joined the rest of the group and asked my friend, Cara, "Did you see me leave the Queen's Chamber?" She said yes. I asked her,

"Did you see me enter the King's Chamber?" Again, she said yes. I never worked out how that had happened.

Years later I met with my spiritual teacher, John-Roger, and he said, "Obviously you weren't where you were." He told me all about the Cheops Pyramid, and then he said, "If you really want to experience its energy you need to climb on the outside of it." Since then, I've climbed on top of it four times. On April 21, the vernal equinox, I was climbing up the outside with four others. For the first half of the climb it felt like something was trying to pull me off and throw me down. I felt concerned...it was like being in a dream when you can't run or get any traction on the ground. I continued on regardless, and after halfway up it felt like something was lifting me up, which made climbing effortless.

Another experience I had at the pyramids was at the Chephren Pyramid. Every morning I would get up early at sunrise and go for a run. At the base of the Chephren Pyramid, facing the sphinx, there are remnants of another structure. One morning, during my run, I sat on a stairway to meditate, and when I opened my eyes I saw the pyramids as they used to be, with people milling around, going through their "ordinary" day in the dress of the time. The experience was real, as though I were actually back in that time. The pyramids were all bright primary colors, and the capstone of the Cheops Pyramid was solid gold.

LAUREN NEMETH GONZALEZ
Co-owner of Greywolf Ministries
Otis, Oregon, United States

When I left my body, I experienced invisible and true palpitations of the soul screaming to know what is real. I felt the authenticity of beaming white light all around me, realizing that in the depths of the soul and spirit lie all that is, and all that ever will be. There was a complete awakening of trust. It felt as though I had been lifted to the heavens. Mother Earth granted her sweet divinity of nature within my bones, my flesh, my mind, and my heart, blowing her fresh air, her branches of grace, her flowering scents of gardenias all around me, gentling carrying me to all that is, and all that will be. A mission of truth, in my deepest vulnerability, awakened my eyes. I could see. I could see truth, honesty, and love. I felt a blanket of serene calm, as if the dragonflies had descended upon me, and with each flutter of their delicate wings carried all my worries to the breeze. That same breeze took all my doubt, grief, and pain away.

As I rose to the swirling heavens in flowering clouds of white light, my soul revealed all that is within me. I was given the gift of my Self, of complete awareness, awakening from the depths of invisible denial. I opened my eyes and saw my greatest and most overwhelming emotion of love and joy through the eyes of my highest self, seeing with not only my eyes, but also my heart. In these moments I realized that all is connected in a divine, intense, and beautiful universe of supernova frequencies and vibrations. I heard a revelation of sounds, perfectly tuned in to the six senses that have been so beautifully gifted to each of us. I circled Mother Earth in profound and humble compassion, thanking her for the enormous and awesome gift of beautiful life.

I experienced all of this when I crossed over for three seconds, even though it seemed like hours. I was in the hospital, and leaving my body was the most heavenly and life changing experience I have had to date.

United in Light

The following stories reveal how four family members came together, after each endured a personal tragedy, to form a not-for-profit organization in order to help others in their community. This book is dedicated to the wonderful charity they formed: Infinite Love.

POOJA CHUGANI
McAllen, Texas, United States

I always had a feeling inside that there was something more to life. In a sense I had a great life—two wonderful kids, a husband, a successful business, a house—but even with all the trappings of what one might call "success" I found that life felt empty and meaningless. Often I would ask God, "What am I doing here? What is the point of all of this?"

One day, I went to meditate with a friend, and while there I met a lady called Giovanna. We clicked right away and I discovered that she works at a nonprofit organization that helps at-risk youth and had friends who worked with homeless people. A spark ignited in my heart, although I didn't know why at the time.

One day, I stumbled across the movie *Conversations with God*, which was the story of spiritual author Neale Donald Walsch's life and how he was homeless before he wrote the *Conversations with God* books that went on to sell millions of copies. The movie shook me to my core, particularly the scene where Mr. Walsch, with tears in his eyes, was forced to eat a half-eaten sandwich he found in a dumpster out of sheer hunger and desperation. It was what moved me to see what I could do to reach out to homeless populations in my hometown. I remembered Giovanna and invited her to come have a chat with me and my daughter. At that first meeting, we spontaneously decided to go to the local park where we knew the homeless people hung out. It was cold, starting to get dark, and I have to admit that I felt scared. I wondered in the back of my mind whether they might be doing drugs, or whether they might rob us. Nevertheless, we put our fears aside, ventured into the park, and found it in our hearts to give pizzas, blankets, and drinks to a group of homeless people. It felt really good, and that was our first taste of helping the homeless.

Around this time, our nephew, Vishal, passed away at age 30 after a battle with cancer that began when he was 18 years old. He had noticed a little bump on his leg, got it checked out, and the doctor diagnosed it as cancer. That was devastating news for the whole family. We all thought, *How can a member of our family that has a temple and prays regularly get cancer? How can something so terrible happen to us?* We prayed and prayed, but the cancer never went away. Vishal had countless operations and strong bouts of chemotherapy between the ages of 18 and 30. Then the cancer spread to his lungs and he had pieces removed. Despite all of this, he constantly had a smile on his face, and nobody outside of his immediate friends and family would ever have guessed he had cancer. He partied hard too, and loved to have fun.

At his funeral we played a playlist he had created with his sister for his funeral. It was composed of all his favorite Beatles songs, including one of our favorites, "All You Need is Love." He had also wanted everyone to down a tequila shot, and had even asked us to put some on his lips. It was a very emotional day, and the amount of people who turned up was unbelievable. The whole funeral hall was packed full, and there were even people spilling out onto the street. Countless people approached Vishal's mom saying how he had given so much love to them, and helped them in ways for which they expressed deep gratitude. No one in the family knew about these random acts of kindness, as he kept them to himself. He had passed away on Valentine's Day, 2011.

A month later, in March, I traveled to India with my twin sisters, Malka and Alka. On the trip we met some very powerful spiritual teachers whom people typically do not get to see so easily. There was one guru—Radha Swami—who is very famous in India and always has crowds of people wanting to see him. He happened to walk right past us in the temple and looked right into our eyes, to our souls. We took that as a huge blessing. Then we went to the town of Bangalore and meditated in a pyramid-shaped room with amazing energy. Each of us went very deep into meditation. In the bookshop after, we purchased half a suitcase full of Radha Swami's books, and they all described the importance of meditation. When we returned from India I held a meeting in my house, and we discussed how we all wanted to start meditating. That's how our meditation group began, and we initially held it in Malka's house. Before long more and more people turned up to join in with no effort or persuading on our part.

This is when I started playing with the idea of forming a non-profit organization in memory of Vishal. We knew we had to include "love" in its name, as Vishal was all about love. The whole family brainstormed a name. Then, in Divine timing, Nipun sent me a book by his sister-in-law, Pavi Mehta, called *Infinite Vision*. As I looked at it, suddenly it came to me like a lightning bolt, and I said, "I've got it! Infinite Love!" We went to our cousin Geeta's office to decide upon the logo, and I said, "Because it's called Infinite Love, the logo has to include an infinity sign." Then Malka said, "Don't you remember that my son has an infinity symbol tattooed on his arm?" I said, "Yes." And then Malka said, "And do you remember why he has it?" I looked blank so Malka continued. "He got the tattoo done in memory of Vishal because when he was alive he always signed off with an "8" or an infinity sign on his paintings."

One year after Vishal's death, on Valentine's Day 2012, Malka, Alka, Geeta, and I went to my aunt's house to commemorate his one-year death anniversary. While there we announced the formation of Infinite Love in memory of Vishal. Everybody placed a red rose by his photo, and it felt like he was smiling down on all of us.

Then the miracles and synchronicities started to happen to an even greater degree than before. Someone gave us an office space for our weekly meditation groups and didn't charge us for using it. The group began with only 15 people, and then it grew and grew until the space started to get tight. Just when we were wondering what to do, the people who owned the office space came to see us and announced that the business next door wanted to expand into our space. They said they had another space elsewhere that was bigger and that we could use that instead. I loved the new venue as soon as I entered. Since acquiring the larger space, we now have 50 to 60 people attending our meditation group every week. We also have monthly Sunday Awakening events where renowned speakers come to Infinite Love to share their empowering messages with whomever would like to listen in the community. We would not have been able to expand in this way without being gifted with the larger space.

Forming Infinite Love has been catalytic in my own happiness. It's an expression of who I am. Since we began I've received an incredible amount of love. The people in our community always thank us, but I thank them back, as they radiate so much love and light and many of them volunteer to help with our events and feeding the homeless people in the park. Because of the work we do, giving and helping others, I feel like I'm personally receiving an abundance of healing. It's very exciting to watch, and I'm always thinking about how Infinite Love can expand.

MALKA SHIVDASANI
McAllen, Texas, United States

Back in 2006 our life was pretty normal. My husband and I have two children, a successful business, and the house of our dreams. Life seemed to be wonderful, but at the same time I had a feeling of emptiness inside.

Then on July 29, 2006, I received a phone call at 3:30 a.m. that would change everything. It was my nephew, Vishal. He told me that my son, Vik, had fallen off his balcony in Houston and that we needed to get there immediately. At this time Vik was 22, and in his last year of undergrad school. I was startled, and my husband had to hold me down as I was trembling so much. It felt as though my soul knew what I would encounter in the coming months and years. We were both in shock and couldn't function. Thank God that my daughter Karina was there. She took over and got us out on the first flight to Houston.

At this point all we knew was that Vishal had gone to Vik's place for the weekend with their other cousins to celebrate Vishal's current clean bill of health from cancer. When we arrived at the hospital the doctors told us he had a spinal cord injury and needed to have surgery. He had fallen from the third-floor balcony, 30 feet down, and he was paralyzed from the waist down. I could not comprehend that fact. The surgery took five hours and all the while my husband, our families, and I prayed and prayed. After the surgery the doctor said, "It's a miracle his spinal cord was not severed inside. He has a 3- to 5-percent chance of walking again. If his spinal cord had been severed he would definitely never be able to walk again."

At that time I didn't understand that every situation that comes to us is a lesson that needs to be mastered. I had to learn to let go and let God handle it. At first, it was very hard to surrender completely because we always want to be in control. I was afraid of what God had in store for Vik and could not accept it! We traveled all around the world to find treatments to cure Vik's paralysis. Unfortunately, all the treatments failed. I have since learned that controlling any situation is going against the flow of the Universe. I realized that going against God's plan causes us a lot of suffering, but I guess everything is a process. Then one day, three and a half years after Vik was in a wheelchair, I finally surrendered Vik to God and said, "It's Your will...he's Your son before he's my son... You love him even more than I do." Soon after that, everything changed. Vik decided to go back to Houston to study, and complete a CPA certification course. My life and his life are so connected, and for us to grow we had to be separate. As soon as he announced that he wanted to go back to Houston, I saw the twinkle return to his eyes.

Then, in 2011, Vishal passed away from cancer. We all suffered extensively. He was an earth angel and left us a message that

LOVE heals everything. I have now realized that the tragedies we face in life are blessings in disguise, because the pain breaks us open to experience the fullness we are meant to be, and connects us with our inner soul's path. Our life purpose is to find our true selves or our true essence, which is Love, and then to spread it to everyone around us to help them see their own light and learn to shine it brighter and brighter. Infinite Love has been a great healer for all of us. My sisters and I can help people through what we all have experienced. My awakening has led me to appreciate life with a totally new perspective. It has made me more compassionate, and my heart is now wide open, in order to give more love to the world. I have discovered myself and my purpose, and it has helped me heal a great deal. I see the blessings that God brings our way every day, and I am so grateful. Vik is now a comedian, he is writing a book, and he is on his way to becoming a motivational speaker! I am really excited to watch his life and all the magic that is coming his way!

ALKA VASWANI
McAllen, Texas, United States

For me everything started with my divorce, in 2006, and that led to my initial awakening. I separated from my husband and started a new life for myself. It was difficult because I had been married for 26 years and at that time I had a 20-year-old daughter. It was like learning to live again. At the age of 18 I had gone through an Indian arranged marriage, so I had left my father's house to go straight into living in my husband's house. Then, 26 years later, I was suddenly by myself.

Like a baby I had to learn to crawl and start walking...taking little steps in order to live again. But little did I know that God had a plan for me and life was only just beginning, not ending. Within the last six years I have fallen down and stood up again, and every time I fall I stand up stronger and taller. Today I am the best I can be, but now I don't need to fall anymore in order to be that person.

In our hearts Pooja, Alka, Geeta, and I wanted to do something to help others. We had been hurt and wanted to let others know that there is life after pain, losing somebody, going through a divorce...any tragic event. Through our work with Infinite Love, we are the message that God wants to give others. He is using us as His instruments, and we only do what we need to do.

Since the formation of Infinite Love, I am a more compassionate person. I have learned that when we help others it's a selfish act: really we are helping and healing ourselves. When you act out of love then you become love. Loving others helps us to become true love, and this helps us grow into a softer person. My tragic event was going through a mentally and verbally abusive marriage.

Now I find myself giving love and receiving love on a daily basis. I'm so excited because this is just the beginning of Infinite Love.

Within Infinite Love, each of us bring our different strengths. I play a Public Relations role because I know a lot of people, and it's easy for me to get the word out about the meditation group and the Sunday Awakening events.

GEETA THADANI
McAllen, Texas, United States

My husband passed away from bladder cancer in 2007. For about a year I was in denial, busy dealing with the kids, our business, and the life changes I faced. Then, when I realized what had happened and it began to sink in, I started going downhill. My life turned upside-down. I began to feel very lonely and the reality that my husband wasn't here with me anymore hit home. Soon I fell into a deep depression, and I couldn't eat or sleep. I closed down the business because I couldn't manage it by myself. My depression quickly worsened.

Around the date of my husband's third death anniversary I noticed my daughter becoming a little depressed. That motivated me to get better. I looked at my husband's photo in my temple and told him I promised I would get back to my old self, which was outgoing and strong. I started going out again in a bid to stop being a zombie. I read inspirational books and listened to speeches by spiritual people. Slowly I felt better.

One day I went to meditate at Malka's house and we saw the movie *Conversations with God*. That triggered something within all of us, and we decided we wanted to help the homeless. However, my true passion was to help cancer patients and their families. I went to Texas Oncology and talked to the administrator, unsure how I would handle entering a cancer center for the first time since my husband had passed away. The administrator was very welcoming. Through Infinite Love we help cancer patients with their rent money or electricity bills, as many cannot afford to pay their usual bills while they're undergoing expensive chemotherapy treatment. We also serve lunch daily to the chemotherapy patients, because there's no cafeteria at the cancer center, and they get hungry. We only serve a little sandwich but that means so much to them.

The time I spend at the cancer center motivates me a great deal, and when I serve the patients their lunch and give them a smile, it also makes me smile. The patients appreciate it hugely. I now feel like I'm serving my purpose. Talking to the patients for a couple of minutes helps them to feel human again.

Even though I don't have my husband anymore, my emptiness is now filled. Giving to others in need has helped me to heal faster than I would have done otherwise. I feel great when I get up in the morning and know I have to go to the cancer center. It has become a key part of my life.

And so Infinite Love was formed, and this book is dedicated to the beautiful women who formed it, their heart-centered work, and their Light-filled cousin who passed away from a rare form of cancer at the age of 30.

Index

Akashic Records, 66-67

Alexander, Joseph, 121-125

angels, being protected by, 151-161

animals, Spirit and, 101-112

Arencibia, Victor, 146-149

awakenings, spiritual, 37-86

birds, Spirit and, 101-112

Bradley, K.T., 115-118

Chugani, Pooja, 233-236

Concepcion, Sandra Nicole, 134-141

consciousness, the Light and, 60

dark night of the soul, 13

Davis, Hannah M., 173-179

death, fear of, 61-62

DellaValle, Marie Serio, 152-156

Dent, Angela, 96, 102-103, 165-167

Dinner, David, 30-32

divine, surrendering to the, 61

Donbavand, Samatha, 187-190

dream state, seeing Spirit in, 115-118

Edwards, Debbie, 190-202

Eiken-Bentley, Sara, 172

energy flashes, psychic, 71

Erickson, Kriss, 205-208

essence, the Light, 80-86

eternity, looking at the field of, 63-64

experiences, subtle, 203-224

fairley, Molly Ann, 66-67

fear of death, 61-62

Franks, Nathalie, 98-100

Gabbitas, Tricia, 173, 229

Goldstein, Pamela, 103-107

Gonzalez, Lauren Nemeth, 27-30, 231-232

Goodwin, Gail Lynne, 55-58

gratitude, state of endless, 66

Green, Heather Wade, 15-26

Harvey, Richard, 60-66

Hayes, Deborah Jayne, 107-109

healing in the Light, 187-190

healing, 169-179

Henderson, Alison, 167-168

Hunting, Paul, 211-216

Jacot, Raederle Phoenix Lydell West, 34-35

Jesus and the Masters, 127-149

Jones, Kimberly, 49-55

Keating, Roisheen, 33, 171

Keating, Roisheen, 33

lives, past, 181-202

Longhurst, Brian, 128-131

Mackenzie, Jennifer, 96-97, 115-116

memories, subconscious, 184-185

messages
from Spirit, 87-100
from synchronicity, 87-100

miracles, 62-63

Moore, Glenn, 216-224

moving toward the light, 15-26

ordinary world, fascination with the, 65

out-of-body experiences, 225-241

owls, 102-103

passion, the power of, 223-224

past lives, 69-71, 181-202

Penn, Shirah S., 58-59

premonitions, 163-168

Proctor, Dina, 39-47

psychic energy flashes, 71

Ratcliffe-Feterson, David,
      80-96

Roads, Michael, 73-80

Sauboorah, Sharon May,
      119-120, 160-161

Schwarzwald, Gabrielle, 80-86

Sebastian, Lauren, 109-110

seeing the light, 13-35

Segal, Cynthia, 48-49

Seretan, Stephen, 209-210

Shivdasani, Malka, 236-238

Sievernich, Melanie, 184-187

Slaw, Suzanne, 156-160

Spirit,
      messages from, 87-100
      seeing, 113-125
      synchronicity of, 80-86

spirits, being protected by,
      151-161

spiritual awakenings, 37-86

St-Pierre, Marilyn, 26-27

subconscious memories,
      184-185

subtle experiences, 203-224

synchronicity, messages from,
      87-100

Thadani, Geeta, 239-241

Tillman, Terry, 111-112,
      131-134, 229-231

transformation, light of the,
      65-66

Vaswani, Akla, 238-239

Waterborn, Richard, 142-146

About the Author

Keidi Keating experienced a sudden spiritual awakening at the age of 30, after a series of transformational healing sessions. One night, an orb of glowing white light appeared in her bedroom and instructed her to put together a book of Light to assist and support others on their journeys to enlightenment. So, following Divine guidance, which showed up as white butterflies, auspicious number combinations, and intense dreams, she gathered some of the planet's greatest spiritual teachers and authors to contribute chapters. Three years later, after a lot of hard work and synchronistic magic, *The Light* spilled its rays to readers, attracting international publishing offers almost immediately! Keidi now speaks at spirit-related events, and she continues to write books that empower people to awaken their Divine inner Light. She currently lives in Ketchum, Idaho. Her Website is *www. keidikeating.com.*

Help us shine the Light far and wide by contributing your own Experiences of the Light story to a future book.

E-mail **info@thelightnetwork.com**.